Men Only

kiss my palate

GWEN HALL

Published by:
R&R Publications Marketing Pty Ltd
ABN 78 348 105 138
12 Edward Street,
Brunswick Victoria 3056
Australia
Phone: (61 3) 9381 2199
Fax: (61 3) 9381 2689
Australia wide toll-free: 1 800 063 296
E-mail: info@randrpublications.com.au
Website: www.randrpublications.com.au

Men Only: Kiss My Palate
Author: Gwen Hall

Publisher: Richard Carroll
Production Manager: Anthony Carroll
Food Photography: Craig Cranko and
Brent Parker Jones
Food Stylist: Jenny Fanshaw and
Neil Hargreaves
Graphic Designer: Elain Wei Voon Loh
Cover Designer: Lucy Adams

Includes index
ISBN 1 74022 516 3
EAN 9 781740 225 168

This edition printed July 2005
Computer typeset in AGaramond,
Shelley Allegro, Pinxit Astroll and
F2 FSimbolico.

Printed in China by:
Max Production Printing Ltd

Distributed in the United States by:
CPG Distribution Inc.
PO Box 190694
Miami Beach. Fl 33119
Phone: 305 538 2495
Fax: 305 538 2504
e-mail: cpgdistribution@juno.com

SHRIMP IN ORANGE SAUCE (recipe on page 32)

SESAME CHICKEN SALAD (recipe on page 157)

Contents

Introduction

Men Only: Kiss My Palate is more than a cookbook. It is a guidebook to romantic entertaining. It includes tips on libations that will complement your meal and an ambience that will engage all of your senses and capture the subliminal mood-altering activities that will help to keep relationships alive. This book has everything to create a perfect evening and much more.

Men Only: Kiss My Palate has all of the information a novice or experienced male chef will need to prepare dinners that make an evening special for any couple. By making her feel like she is the only woman in the world, creating a night that neither of you will forget, you can turn this night into a memorable morning. This cookbook has breakfast suggestions for that morning after. Encore menus are also included as she *will be back*.

For centuries oysters, caviar, asparagus, truffles and honey have been said to be aphrodisiacs. Beef, chocolate, mushrooms and artichokes have been added to this list. Is the way to a woman's heart through her stomach? Do aphrodisiacs really work? When taken with belief and in the spirit of mutual desire, they guarantee stimulation of the most jaded paramour and gourmet. After a perfect meal, men and women are more susceptible to the ecstasy of lovemaking than at any other time.

"*Without bread, Without wine, Love is nothing.*"

French proverb

Chapter 1: Getting Started

1

"A toast to bread, for without bread, there would be no toast"

Author Unknown

1.1 BREAKING DOWN BARRIERS BY BREAKING BREAD

Men may not have the answers to life's mysterious questions, like, "What is humanity's place in the cosmos?", "Is there life after death?", "How can I change the world?", "What is the meaning of life?", and most importantly, "How do I get a smoking-hot girlfriend who is great looking?" Add culinary skills to humor and charisma and you land a dream date, potentially making a paradigm shift in your relationship from friends to lovers. Just like the great line by Al Capone (Robert De Niro) in *The Untouchables*, you get further with a kind word and a gun than just a kind word. These dinners will give the male rock-solid confidence in serving a perfect meal: Act 1 of a great evening.

Association between food and romance has been firmly established for centuries. This cookbook is a reminder of the added pleasures that can be derived from food. It is not what food brings to you; it is what you bring to the food.

It is time for nice guys to start finishing first. Men who can cook are getting the woman who wants to be romanced. Now real men can add culinary arts to their lists of skills. When today's woman escaped from the kitchen and took up power lunches, fast food and grocery store take-out, she also decided to accept invitations to a man's home where he is in the kitchen cooking.

Do women respond positively to an invitation to dinner at your house? Absolutely!!!

"Cooking for someone is like love —

it should be entered into with abandon, or not at all"

Harriet Van Horne

1.2 THE BENEFITS OF SEDUCTIVE DINNERS

The men, who include romantic cooking in their backpack of bedroom skills, tell us they do it for several reasons. In no order of importance they are:

♡ Control the environment

♡ Lower a woman's resistance

♡ Save money

♡ Impress the unimpressable woman

Control the Environment

If a woman accepts a dinner date at your home, she probably wants to get to know you. In a restaurant that is difficult. There you are competing with the waiters, the couple next to you who brought their six-year-old to a five-star restaurant, and her ex-lover who just walked through the door with a twenty-something woman in a clingy dress slit to the navel. Or worse, your ex-lover greets you at the table, gives you a hug and says "Let's get together soon".

At home you have control of the environment and mood. Once you have a date in your home, don't forget to turn the volume down on the answering machine and shut off your cell phone. Put a sign on the door saying "Not at Home" and devote three or four hours to learning more about the woman at your dining room or kitchen table. It will pay off for both of you, as you won't start the evening with a *dream and wake up with reality*.

> *"One cannot think well, love well, sleep well, if one has not dined well."*
>
> Virginia Wolf

Lower a Woman's Resistance

We are not talking about Spanish Fly in the wine. Put a woman in an environment where you show that you really care; put her first and she will surrender. Look at the personal ads: The men who add "romantic" in their ad, along with "candlelit dinners", get responses. However, many of these ads offer false advertising. A candlelit dinner of a slightly burned steak served on plastic plates isn't very romantic; especially when you learn over wine that your date is a vegetarian. Prepare a menu that is simple yet good, food that she won't have to hide in her handbag; ask if it is okay to have a truly decadent dessert and soon she will be asking for seconds, as she straightens her clothes.

Save Money

The cost of eating at home is less than eating at a restaurant. But don't go cheap on the home-cooked meal. A $20 bottle of wine from the liquor store costs at least $30 and more in an upscale restaurant. Fresh seafood and prime beef are expensive, but are a fraction of what you would pay if you dined out. You can spend a third less by dining at home. Invest the savings in something special for her, like fresh flowers or a new CD. One way to a woman's heart is *buying an unanticipated gift at an unexpected time.*

"Cooking is a lot like making love. It just takes a little longer to clean up."

Michael Tucker

Impress the Unimpressible

You've met a woman you'd like to know and she is putting you on hold. Offer to cook dinner for her and you will be spending more time together. Throw in a romantic setting and good champagne and your evening may progress from a "good night" kiss to "good morning" kiss. When you call her for an encore evening, she will give her prize opening night theatre ticket to a friend, saying "I have to see about a guy", and spend the evening with you.

Key Points

♡ Your first "dinner and a movie" date can be in your home. Renting several movies is cheaper than tickets for a non-matinee movie.

♡ Real men may not eat quiche, but they can prepare it after a sleepover.

♡ The more expensive the wine, the more likely your evening of erotic gastronomy will go from the kitchen through the dining room to the bedroom.

♡ If cooking steak is the best thing you do, specifically ask if she eats red meat.

♡ A great dinner, with complementary libations, is going to cost you. Remember the benefits of your investment.

♡ Cooking for her will impress her as much as what you cook.

♡ Some guy is going to be in the kitchen with Dinah or Sarah or Libby, and it might as well be you.

♡ Great evenings start with a bottle of wine for the cook, sharing cooking tasks, and having her change the CD and arranging the fresh flowers while you are both having an interesting conversation.

♡ The money you spend working out in the gym and building bulging muscles could be better spent on cooking classes. Women actually prefer men with ordinary physiques and you will have a great time learning to cook. More importantly, you may get a date.

1.3 A Well-Equipped Kitchen is Just as Important as a Well-Equipped Man

If additional kitchen utensils are needed to prepare a meal, they will be included on the grocery lists that are with each menu.

In case you were concerned, the size of your kitchen is not important. It is how you use it that counts. As long as two people can spoon in the kitchen, you can prepare a romantic meal. Cooking in that postage-stamp kitchen you will get you close, get you crazy and get you into it.

I said to my wife,
"Where do you want to go for your anniversary?"
She said, "I want to go somewhere I've never been before."
I said, "Try the kitchen."

Henry Youngman

The following items are key to planning seductive meals

♡ 1 corkscrew

♡ 1 non-stick skillet

♡ 2 saucepans, 1 small and 1 medium

♡ 1–2 quart baking dish

♡ 2–3 good knives (chef's knife, paring knife and bread knife)

♡ 1 vegetable peeler

♡ 1 chopping board

♡ 1 colander (spaghetti strainer)

♡ 1 food processor or blender

♡ 1 set measuring spoons

♡ 1 set measuring cups

♡ 2 mixing bowls, small and medium

♡ 1 coffee maker or espresso machine

♡ 1 coffee grinder (if you buy whole beans)

♡ 1 pepper grinder

♡ 1 grill, the George Foreman-type or outdoor grill or indoor Jenn-Aire

♡ 1 timer

♡ 1 toaster

♡ a set of kitchen utensils (spatulas, slotted spoons, whisk)

♡ 2 kitchen towels

♡ 2 wash cloths

♡ 2 pot holders

♡ 1 can opener

Table Setting

There is nothing romantic about drinking wine from a beer mug, eating veal scaloppine off a cheap chipped plate, eating soup out of matching margarine containers or using plastic utensils from your favorite fast-food restaurant. Remember, this is an investment in seduction, and the benefits you will receive in return. Buy four of everything just in case a plate breaks while you are serving dinner. If she stays over, you will want clean plates for breakfast. If you need assistance in making these purchases, invite a female friend or relative to go with you. You can also get assistance from the department store personal shopper or sales associate in the China department. You will receive excellent advice and you may get a date.

Invest in:

♡ 4 place settings of dishes

♡ 2 serving bowls

♡ 4 soup bowls

♡ creamer and sugar bowl

♡ 4 wine glasses

♡ 4 champagne flutes

♡ 4 water glasses

♡ 4 place settings of heavy stainless flatware

♡ 1 tablecloth or 4 attractive place mats and 4 napkins

♡ salt and pepper shakers

♡ 2 candleholders and candles

♡ 1 vase for fresh flowers

At department and discount stores, you can buy a set of dishes that includes 4 place settings plus soup bowls and serving dishes.

Mood-Setting Equipment

♡ Dimmers for every room in the house

♡ Go to your favorite music store and ask for advice on romantic music. You know by now, you may get a date. Some possibilities are Dubussy (classical), Andrew Bocelli (opera), Kenny G (saxophone), Enya and Yanni (new age), George Winston (piano), blues and jazz.

♡ A clean home: women sometimes break up with guys when they find germs in the kitchen sink that are starting a fight with the mold in the refrigerator.

First impressions always count the most. After all the work you have gone to planning and preparing this meal, be sure that you are ready to warmly welcome her. Cooking is messy if you do it right. Clean your kitchen after preparing what you can, before she arrives. The rest of your house needs attention too. If cleaning isn't your thing, hire someone to do it for you.

Key Points

♡ Real men do have kitchen utensils that are the same color or complementary colors. Black and stainless steel are very manly looking.

♡ Don't alphabetize your spices or straighten the hand towels each time she puts them back. She is looking for someone who isn't a slob, but also someone who is not obsessive-compulsive.

♡ Don't dim all lights before your date arrives or she will feel she is walking into a sex trap.

♡ The first date should be more casual, less planned and the ending of the evening undetermined. Always have clean sheets just in case.

♡ Encore dinners are times for planned romance. Gone is the tension of "will we do it?" The only question is, "when?"

♡ All senses need to be satisfied at once. She will *see* the flowers on the table, *smell* the wonderful food you are cooking, *hear* music that flows through the air, *feel* the warmth of your welcome and *taste* the wine immediately offered upon arrival. (Have the wine bottle open before she arrives.)

Bathroom Investments

♡ Kama Sutra, a bath oil that smells and tastes good (not intended for drinking)

♡ 1 scented candle

♡ soft hand and bath towels

♡ Kleenex, toilet paper and hand lotion

♡ an extra toothbrush, toothpaste and mouthwash

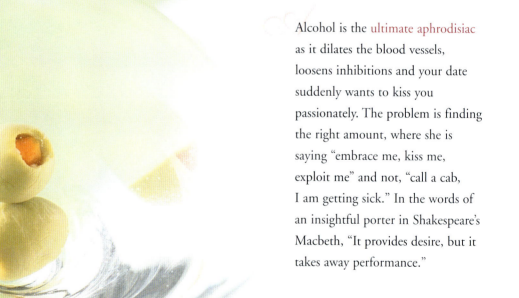

Chapter 2: Marinating Dates

2

"The martini—
the quintessential American cocktail,
the crowning jewel of civilized decadence…"

Anonymous

Alcohol is the ultimate aphrodisiac as it dilates the blood vessels, loosens inhibitions and your date suddenly wants to kiss you passionately. The problem is finding the right amount, where she is saying "embrace me, kiss me, exploit me" and not, "call a cab, I am getting sick." In the words of an insightful porter in Shakespeare's Macbeth, "It provides desire, but it takes away performance."

"No. I mean really dry.
I want to see the dust on my olives."

Anonymous

2.1 DRINKING THE STARS

"Champagne, the real thing, is produced only in the Champagne region of France. All others, no matter how delicious, are sparkling wines" (Wally's Wine World Newsletter). Champagne prompted Dom Perignon to remark, "Oh come quickly, I am drinking the stars!"

"The French have convinced us that we cannot have a serious celebration without a bottle of champagne" (author unknown). Champagne pairs well with seafood dishes or fresh fruit. Light, dry champagnes are good starters and also go well with desserts. There are all ranges of sweetness.

There are scores of fine champagnes, ranging in price from $25 to $200 plus.

Champagne Terms

Dry means not sweet.

Brut is the driest.

Extra dry denotes a touch of sweetness. Slightly sweeter than brut.

Demi-sec or Cremant is a sweeter, creamy style appropriate for dessert.

Champagne Savvy

Serve champagne in tall, narrow flutes to make the most of the bubbles. It also helps keep the champagne effervescent longer. Both champagne and sparkling wines should be served very cold: 39°–50°F. Put the bottle in the refrigerator at least 2 hours before serving.

2.2 WINE, WOMEN AND SEX

Wine makes the experience of a good meal even more enjoyable. Wine is a spice adding another dimension to each meal. It is fun to think about, and each new bottle can be a surprise. "Wine makes every meal an occasion, every table more elegant, every day more civilized" (Andre Simon).

You've invited a wine connoisseur over for dinner and you are wine connoisseur challenged. Here is a crash course on *what you have always wanted to know about wine but were afraid to ask.*

Hold your wine glass by the stem and slowly swirl the wine. Observe the color of the wine. Take a deep whiff of the wine. Finally, you get to taste the wine. Then exalt brilliant comments like "very complex", "interesting" or "different." That's it. A wine connoisseur will use words like "racy", "full-bodied", and "explosive finish." Your response could then be "hmmm" or "are you still talking about the wine?" To keep conversation light, you could add "this wine has great clarity or did I already drink it?"

While there are recommended wine and food combinations, you can also drink wines that taste good to you with food you like to eat. Ask the grocer or liquor store personnel for the best picks at the best price. You will get good advice and maybe a date. Experiment with new wine and food combinations, deviating from the standard combinations of red wine with beef, and white wine with chicken and fish. It's just like dating: when it doesn't work out, try a new combination of wine and food. Eventually you will find the right one (and we aren't just talking about the wine).

"Wine and women...
May we always have a taste for both."

Author unknown

Wine and Food

Food courses usually go from the lightest to the heaviest, and so do the wines. Champagne is a nice way to start. Then to light white wines, heavier white wines, light red wines and finally heavier red wines. If you're having both dry and sweet wines, the order is usually dry first, then sweet.

*Suggestions for serving wines from different regions at the same meal.

♡ Chilled wines come before room-temperature wines.

♡ Younger wines are served before older ones.

♡ Lighter wines come before heavier, coarser ones.

♡ White wines before reds.

♡ Red wines before sweet white wines (unless the sweet white wine has been served as an aperitif).

Pairing Wine and Food: A Handbook for All Cuisines. by Linda Johnson-Bell, by permission of Burford Books, Inc.

Dessert Wines

When serving a dessert with a dessert wine, the wine should be slightly sweeter. If serving fruit or cake, a white dessert wine such as late-harvest muscat, sauternes, and sauvignon blanc go well. If serving chocolate, cabernet sauvignon and port are good. Or, skip the dessert and just serve a sweet wine as dessert. Ice wine is a great dessert substitute; it is usually more expensive than other wines.

*"As in lovemaking, reading is a damn poor substitute
for experience in the gentle art of (wine) tasting.
It is one of those things you find out by yourself."*

James Norwood Pratt

"*Happiness is a dry martini and a good woman… Or a bad woman.*"

George Burns

> *"Wine, madam, is God's next best gift to man."*
>
> Ambrose Bierce

Wine Savvy

Open a bottle thirty minutes before serving so the wine will have breathing time. This is especially beneficial to young red wines. Red wines are served at room temperature and white wines are chilled. Chilled means thirty minutes in the refrigerator and served, or refrigerate until cold and then remove from refrigerator thirty minutes before serving.

2.3 MARTINIS

Baseball is America's pastime, football is America's sport and the martini is the quintessential American cocktail.

This cocktail represents "everything from sophistication to depravity, elegance to wild abandon. Sometimes called 'silver bullet', it's clean, it's cold and it always hits the mark" (*The Martini Book-by Sally Ann Berk by permission of Black Dog & Leventhal Publishers Inc.*). The martini has been a popular drink from the moment it was born. It could be its simplicity; gin or vodka, and vermouth and olives or a lemon twist are all you need to create a martini. The martini glass has an appealing design that is captivating. In the very popular martini bars, contemporary and classic martinis are served.

A popular classic is The Dirty, using vodka or gin, and vermouth and olive juice. The Cosmopolitan has become a preferred contemporary martini for ladies. A Godiva Chocolate Martini garnished with a cherry is a wonderful after-dinner drink and substitute for dessert.

Martini Savvy

To set up a martini bar, you need special equipment. First purchase martini glasses. If you shake your martinis, buy a shaker. Stainless steel chills a drink uniformly and quickly. If you prefer stirred martinis, purchase a good mixing glass and a long-handled bar spoon. You will also need a cocktail strainer, a cutting board, a knife, an ice bucket, tongs, cocktail napkins and toothpicks. Women will be impressed if you purchase glasses and a shaker that match. Martini glasses can be used as candleholders for a round candle.

Chapter 3: Seductive Dinners

3

There is an old joke: "Should you have sex before dinner?" Answer: "Depends on how crowded the restaurant is." At your home, you don't need to worry about when to have sex; before, during or after the meal depends on the willingness of your lady. When planning to have a romantic evening at your home, you do need to make an investment in seduction. Show your guest a lot of consideration. After she accepts the invitation, and before you plan dinner, be sure to ask if there is a food or drink that she would not like to have for dinner. This will tell you if your dinner guest is a vegetarian or has any food allergies.

Don't get in over your head. Stick to what you know. If you get comfortable making one menu, go ahead and make it – just make sure that you didn't serve it to her best friend last week. Remember, it is always fun to try something new – both in bed and in the kitchen.

Keep it simple. She is dating you, not Emeril Lagasse.

Know your ingredients. Read each recipe completely before your special evening. If you discover an hour before dinner is to be served that the meat was supposed to marinate for 12 hours, you are totally screwed (the kind you will not enjoy).

Know your aphrodisiacs. Aphrodisiacs have been credited with the ability to stimulate love and sex, not necessarily in that order. Almost every food has at one time been believed as an aphrodisiac. Food is sexy, providing you look at it the right way. One's imagination is the most sensuous and powerful aphrodisiac. Most recipes in this cookbook include aphrodisiacs.

"The right diet directs sexual energy into the parts that matter."

Barbara Cartland

Know your grocery store: The best place to shop is a grocery store offering one-stop shopping that includes food, wine/liquor, flowers, deli, gourmet take-out, special occasion cards, decorative items and DVD rentals. The ingredients for all the recipes in this book can be found in any grocery store, without including seldom-used ingredients that you would have to go to gourmet shops to find. Get to know your grocery store personnel and soon they will let you know when special cuts of meat will be on sale and set aside the last bottle of good Merlot that was on sale at an unbelievably low price. The florist will give you tips on how to keep flowers fresh through two or three romantic dinners.

Just as important as planning your menu is seeking advice on the details. Ask your florist what kind of flowers she suggests (you may even get a date with your florist out of it). Ask the sales associate in the liquor section on wine suggestions. And again, you may get a date.

Establish a time-line. Plan ahead how much time every task will take. Save time by cleaning the night before your date. You will also need to grocery shop and actually cook the meal. Do as much as possible before she arrives.

3.1 FIRST DATES

"Good food is so sexy in its way."

James Beard

Simple and Sophisticated Pasta Seductions

When you select recipes that can be prepared easily and quickly, you leave time for other activities. These sophisticated pasta recipes are full of sexy ingredients that will lead to an evening of romance. Rent an Italian movie that you and your *principessa* will enjoy watching after dinner while you have dessert and wine. Ask for movie suggestions at your local rental store and again, you may get a date.

Set the dining room table with a white or red and white checked tablecloth, red or white cloth napkins and red candles. These pasta dinners will provide a plethora of Italian flavors. After dessert, uncork a second bottle of wine or champagne. When your Italian flick is over, head to the hot tub as a finale for your fantasy evening. Candles around the hot tub and plush towels will turn this evening into a scene from *Bull Durham*. Put out all of the candles with water splashed from the hot tub.

Buon appetito!

Penne for Your Dining Thoughts

She's accepted your dinner invitation. Now get to know one another. The best way to learn about your date is to engage her in interesting conversations. The questions in this chapter spark responses followed by lively discussion. Don't just try to find out about her good characteristics. The best stuff is learning one another's faults. Find out what makes her unique. Neither of you is perfect, *but you may be perfect for one another*. Sharing imperfections leads to intimacy and turns a friendship into a love affair.

Women are always interested in a well-educated man. Listening intently to her responses is the greatest compliment and an aphrodisiac. Remembering them will help in planning encore dinners. She will probably ask you the same questions, so anticipate your responses. If her responses are light and humorous, respond in kind. Likewise, if hers are more serious and insightful, don't be flip. In sales, this is called pacing. If she tells you her first boyfriend broke her heart, don't confess that your heart was broken when your favorite baseball team lost the pennant or your #1 football or basketball team is 0 and 3. While both are tragic, mentioning them now will close communication.

Penne for Your Kitchen Thoughts

1 Do you like white meat or dark?

2 Do you prefer red or white wine?

3 Croutons or bacon bits?

4 Coffee or coffee ice cream?

5 Black or red licorice?

6 What is your favorite word? (Include it in a note to her.)

7 Favorite saying? (I'm so upset I could throw-up on my shoes)

8 What store would you max out your credit card in? (a good place
   to shop for her birthday)

9 What do you do when you get bored?

10 At a carnival, would you eat a corn dog or funnel cake?

11 Ever been treated for mallomar's addiction?

12 Do you enjoy cooking?

13 What is your favorite home-cooked meal? (Cook that meal next time.)

14 What was your high today?

15 Did you inherit your wonderful eyes/hands/mouth/nose from your
   mother or your father?

Sautéed scallops, Broiled tomatoes, Almond orzo, Pinot Grigio (Italy) or Chardonnay (Australia), Biscotti, Coffee

BROILED TOMATOES (opposite)

At one time this aphrodisiacal quality was ascribed to the tomato. Reflect on that when preparing this dish.

Rinse and drain tomatoes. Slice in half.

Preheat broiler.

Melt butter in saucepan over medium heat.

Sauté breadcrumbs until golden brown.

Remove from heat and add parsley.

Season with salt and pepper.

Cut ¹/2 inch off top and bottom of tomato.

Sprinkle lightly with salt and black pepper.

Top each tomato with a generous tablespoon of breadcrumb mixture.

Sprinkle with Parmesan cheese. Set tomatoes in a baking dish.

Grill for 5–6 minutes. Tomatoes should be firm and warm with topping golden brown.

Transfer to plate and serve.

*Prep time **5 minutes**   Cook time **5–6 minutes***

BISCOTTI AND COFFEE

Serve biscotti on a salad or dessert plate.

Make coffee.

Eat . . . Drink . . . Enjoy!

SHOPPING LIST

Produce
1 bunch chives, finely minced

2 teaspoons minced garlic

juice of 1 fresh lemon

Grocery
1 box of almond orzo

freshly ground black pepper

Dairy
¹/8 cup whipping cream

4 tablespoons butter

Liquor
¹/8 cup white wine for cooking

pinot grigio or chardonnay to drink

Seafood
1 pound large sea scallops, the freshest you can buy, firm and white, not fishy or sticky

SAUTÉED SCALLOPS WITH ALMOND ORZO (opposite)

Chow! This gutsy pasta will have her lips saying "more, more" and "yes, yes".

Pour a glass of wine for the cook.

Cook orzo according to directions on package and cover.

Melt butter in a large pan, medium-high heat.

Add garlic and chives.

Cook 30 seconds.

Add scallops.

Sauté for 2 minutes on each side.

Add wine and lemon juice.

Cook for 2 more minutes to reduce liquid.

Remove scallops.

Add whipping cream to existing sauce and cook over low heat, constantly stirring.

Return scallops to sauce.

Grind fresh black pepper over scallops.

Reheat orzo.

*Prep time **5 minutes** Cook time **10 minutes***

♡ One hour before: Prepare tomatoes. Cover and refrigerate.

♡ 15–30 minutes before: Prepare scallops. Cook orzo.

♡ 15 minutes before: Broil tomatoes.

♡ Re-heat orzo just before serving.

♡ After eating dinner, make coffee.

SAUTÉED SCALLOPS WITH ALMOND ORZO
(recipe on page 26)

"...the only classical and true way to eat pasta is with gusto."

James Beard

Penne for Your Dinner Thoughts

1 Favorite movie? (Rent it for a future 'dinner and a movie' date.)

2 Favorite restaurant? (Take her there for an encore date or get takea-out from that restaurant and serve it at your place or hers.)

3 Favorite holiday?

4 Favorite drink? (Keep it in your refrigerator.)

5 Favorite foods? (Include in a future dinner menu.)

6 If you had your dream job, what would it be?

7 What would you not do?

8 Rainy day activity?

9 How can I take your heart? After dinner we can see if we have a future.

10 Are there moments when you are moderately attracted to me? If there are, tell me which ones so I can duplicate them.

11 Are your dreams in color? If yes, bet you can't wait to go to sleep.

SAUTÉED SCALLOPS WITH ANGEL HAIR PASTA, SPINACH AND PROSCUITTO SALAD
SAUVIGNON BLANC, FRESH FRUIT, CHOCOLATE AND PORT WINE

SHOPPING LIST

Produce
fresh lemon, cut in wedges

Grocery
2 tablespoons white sesame seeds

Meat
¹/₂ bacon

Seafood
1 pound large sea scallops

Bottle Shop
Sauvignon blanc to drink

Miscellaneous
paper towels

slotted spoon

SHOPPING LIST

Produce
1 lemon

Grocery
1 package angel hair pasta
salt and pepper, to taste
1 tablespoon extra virgin oil

Dairy
1 tablespoon grated Parmesan cheese

Kitchen Equipment
1 zester

SAUTÉED SCALLOPS WITH ANGEL HAIR PASTA (opposite)

Pour a glass of wine for the cook.

Heat sesame seeds in small skillet over medium heat. **Brown** for 6–8 minutes until seeds are browned and toasted. **Stir** constantly.

Rinse and **drain** scallops, then **pat dry** with paper towels.

Cook bacon in skillet. **Remove** bacon as you only want grease for sauteing scallops. Keep bacon grease hot and sauté scallops for 3 minutes on each side–until golden brown.

Using slotted spoon, **remove** scallops from skillet.

Serve on angel hair pasta. **Sprinkle** each scallop with sesame seeds. **Serve** with lemon wedges.

Prep time **15 minutes**   *Cook time* **6–10 minutes**

♡ One hour before: Prepare scallops, but don't sauté yet. Fry bacon.
   Wash and prepare fresh fruit. Make chocolate sauce.

♡ 30 minutes before: Prepare salads.

♡ 15 minutes before: Cook pasta, drain in colander.

♡ 10 minutes before: Sauté scallops.

♡ After dinner, re-heat chocolate sauce and pour into a jug.

ANGEL HAIR PASTA

Cook angel hair pasta according to package directions.

Drain pasta in colander.

Toss with extra virgin oil, lemon zest (from the 1 lemon), salt and pepper.

Sprinkle Parmesan on top.

Produce
2 cups from a bag of fresh, washed spinach
6 thin slices of red onion
2 ounces fresh mushrooms (optional)
1/4 cup dried cranberries (optional)

Grocery
1/3 cup spinach salad dressing
1/2 cup croutons

Meat
4 slices prosciutto, chopped

Dairy
4 tablespoons crumbled blue cheese (optional)
1 hardboiled egg, finely chopped (optional)

SPINACH AND PROSCIUTTO SALAD (opposite)

Spinach has been reputed for ages to maintain strength and restore virility. Spinach is a powerful source of vitamins and minerals, especially iron, which is essential for sexual vigor.

You can purchase packages of spinach and bacon salad, complete with spinach, croutons, bacon bits and dressing. All you have to do is combine the ingredients, heat the dressing and toss.

If you prefer making this salad, here is the basic recipe with optional ingredients, along with instructions. The optional ingredients could be added to the packaged ingredients.

Tear spinach into bite-sized pieces and put in a salad bowl.

Add onion, mushrooms and cranberries, and toss to combine.

Heat dressing in microwave for about 30 seconds.

Pour dressing over salad and toss to coat.

Sprinkle prosciutto, blue cheese, egg and croutons on top.

Prep time **10 minutes**

SHOPPING LIST

Produce
1 cup fresh strawberries
1/2 cup fresh apricots
cantaloupe chunks

Dairy
heavy cream

Frozen Desserts
thick chocolate sauce

Liquor
port to drink

Miscellaneous
bamboo skewers

FRESH FRUIT, CHOCOLATE AND PORT

Wash all fruit.

Leave strawberries whole, cutting off stems.

Pit apricots. Cut cantaloupe into chunks.

Put fruit on skewers.

Heat chocolate sauce on low heat, add 1 tablespoon heavy cream and stir.

Serve skewers on a dessert plate. **Pour** chocolate sauce into a small pitcher so sauce can be poured over the fruit. **Pour** port into wine glasses and serve.

Prep time **15 minutes**

Save some of the fresh fruit for breakfast and serve topped with vanilla yogurt. Using a bar of soap, write a note on the bathroom mirror that you will be serving breakfast in bed.

SPINACH AND PROSCIUTTO SALAD
(recipe on page 30)

Shrimp in Orange Sauce, Angel Hair Pasta, Crusty Bread, with Chardonnay or Pinot Grigio

Shopping List

Produce
1 jalapeño chili

2 green onions, minced

4 tablespoons fresh parsley, chopped

Grocery
salt and pepper

12 ounces angel hair pasta

Seafood
1 pound fresh shrimp, peeled and deveined

Dairy
3/4 stick butter

1 1/2 cups orange juice

3/4 cup whipping cream

Liquor
1/2 cup white wine for recipe

chardonnay or pinot grigio for drinking

Shrimp in Orange Sauce (opposite)

Fresh ingredients make this a delectable dinner.

Pour a glass of wine.

Peel and devein shrimp.

Melt butter and cook shrimp 1 minute per side in a heavy frying-pan, just until pink.

Place shrimp in a bowl and set aside.

Add seeded jalapeño and minced onions.

Sauté 1 minute. Add wine and bring to boil.

Mix in orange juice and cream.

Boil for 10 minutes, stirring occasionally.

Add salt and pepper to taste, about 1/4 teaspoon each.

Cook pasta in boiling water until just tender.

Drain in colander. If sauce has cooled, bring to simmer.

Add shrimp and heat through. Add pasta and toss well.

Top with chopped parsley and serve.

Prep time **15 minutes** *Cook time* **15–20 minutes**

♡ One day before: Clean and devein shrimp, place in refrigerator.

♡ 15 minutes before: Cook shrimp in orange sauce and turn off.

♡ 10 minutes before: Cook pasta; then drain in colander.

♡ 5 minutes before: Slice bread and spread pesto and place in oven for 10 minutes.

SHOPPING LIST

Grocery
fresh pesto with basil

Bakery
1 loaf crusty bread

CRUSTY BREAD WITH PESTO

Preheat oven to 350°F.

Slice bread.

Spread pesto on bread slices.

Bake for 10 minutes.

Put a napkin in a basket.

Place sliced bread in basket.

Prep time **5 minutes**   *Cook time* **10 minutes**

PASTA WITH MUSHROOMS AND GORGONZOLA, CRUSTY BREAD WITH OLIVE OIL, FRESH STRAWBERRY AND BRANDY SUNDAES AND CHIANTI CLASSICO (ITALY)

For this dinner, invite your date to meet you in the kitchen – dress: casual.

Joe bombs when he attempts a "Mad Dog" seduction. His box wine blush selection was worse. He fails miserably when he serves spaghetti from a can. Joe gets turned in to the Health Department because of the mold in his refrigerator. In desperation, he buys a cookbook, tries several recipes on his friends, completes a wine-tasting class and hires a cleaning service. Joe serves this dinner to Caitlin. They are getting married next month.

SHOPPING LIST

Produce
1 onion, chopped
³/4 pound sliced mushrooms
1 teaspoon minced garlic

Grocery
8 ounces whole wheat spaghetti or fettuccine
2 tablespoons olive oil
salt and pepper
¹/2 cup walnuts, chopped

Dairy
¹/2 cup whipping cream
2 ounces Gorgonzola
grated Parmesan

Liquor
¹/4 cup red wine for cooking
Chianti classico to drink

PASTA WITH MUSHROOMS AND GORGONZOLA (opposite)

"Fungi were so highly prized in early Roman times that no mere servant was allowed to cook them. Aristocrats prepared their own mushroom dishes in special silver vessels called *boleteria*. Guests could tell where they stood in their host's esteem by the number and variety of mushroom dishes served them" (Maggie Waldron in *Cold Spaghetti at Midnight*).

Pour a glass of wine for the cook.

Precook spaghetti or fettuccine, according to package directions.

Drain in colander.

Heat oil in heavy large skillet over medium-high heat. **Add** onion and sauté until translucent, about 5 minutes.

Add mushrooms and cook until mushrooms are very tender, stirring frequently (about 5 minutes).

Stir in wine and boil until liquid is reduced to glaze (about 4 minutes).

Mix in cream and bring to boil.

Season with salt and pepper, about ¹/4 teaspoon each.

Add spaghetti to skillet and heat through, stirring constantly.

Stir in Gorgonzola and walnuts.

Sprinkle Parmesan and serve.

*Prep time **10 minutes**   Cook time **20–25 minutes***

"For a plate of spaghetti, he'd leave home.

For another woman? Never!"

Adua Pavarotti

♡ 30 minutes before: Cook spaghetti or fettuccine; drain in colander.

♡ 15 minutes before: Make mushroom sauce.

♡ 10 minutes before: Slice bread and prepare olive oil topped with cracked pepper.

♡ 5 minutes before: Combine pasta and mushroom sauce and reheat.

♡ After dinner: Serve ice cream.

> *"To dream of mushrooms denotes fleeting happiness, to dream you are gathering them, fickleness in a lover or consort."*
>
> Richard Folkard

SHOPPING LIST

Grocery
$^1/_4$ cup olive oil
1 tablespoon balsamic vinegar

Bakery
1 loaf crusty bread

CRUSTY BREAD WITH OLIVE OIL

Slice bread and put in basket lined with a cloth napkin.

Pour olive oil into a small bowl, stir in balsamic vinegar.

Prep time **5 minutes**

Serve toasted leftover bread for breakfast. Also have low-fat margarine and raspberry jam, along with coffee or tea.

SHOPPING LIST

Produce
$^1/_2$ cup stemmed and halved strawberries

Frozen Desserts
1 pint vanilla ice cream

Liquor
4 tablespoons brandy

STRAWBERRY AND BRANDY SUNDAES

Dip 1–2 scoops of ice cream into each bowl.

Top with halved strawberries.

Pour brandy over sundaes and serve.

Without bread all is misery.

William Cobbett

A mutual friend introduces Tom and Margo. After meeting at numerous pubs for drinks and attending several concerts in the park, Tom invites Margo to his place for spaghetti. While Margo is in awe of Tom's homemade spaghetti sauce and wine selections, his well-equipped kitchen impresses her even more. He has two timers, a spaghetti strainer and a spaghetti measurer. This becomes the night of the "spaghetti seduction". In the morning, Tom borrows a line from *Goodbye Girl*, telling Margo that last night was the superbowl of romance. *On a scale of 1–10, Margo scores a 9. He had to deduct 1 point for burping after drinking the wine.*

Penne for Your After Dinner Thoughts

1 How do you like to be kissed?

2 What turns you on or inspires you?

3 What sounds do you love? (Buy that CD for a future evening at your place.)

4 Has your heart been broken?

5 What chance do I have of ending up with you? 1 out of 10? 1 out of a 100? (Hopefully your chances will be better than Jim Carrey's in *Dumb and Dumber* where his chances were 1 in a million. Whatever your chances, always respond, "So you are telling me there is a chance.")

6 Been in love before?

7 Would you like to be rich or pretty?

8 Happy or famous?

9 Travel internationally?

10 Would you like an after-dinner kiss?

11 Let's snuggle naked–nothing will happen, I promise!

Please select just a few questions from the above suggestions, as no one enjoys an evening of interrogation or participating in a research project. The evening progresses, time passes unnoticed as pleasures intensify.

LASAGNA, ITALIAN SALAD, GARLIC BREAD, DARK CHOCOLATE ICE CREAM AND CHARDONNAY

You can pick up lasagna, salad and garlic bread from your favorite Italian restaurant and transfer them to serving dishes. Lasagna can also be purchased in the frozen food section of your grocery store and baked. If you hide the containers, your lady will never know. Or you can cook this recipe.

SHOPPING LIST

Produce
4 tablespoons parsley, chopped

1 cup chopped cooked spinach

Grocery
10 ounces of tomato sauce

3 lasagna noodles

cooking spray

aluminum foil

Dairy
4 ounces of low-fat cottage cheese

1/2 cup Mozzarella, shredded

grated Parmesan cheese

Bakery
1 loaf of garlic bread

Liquor
chardonnay for drinking

LASAGNA (photograph on page 41)

Cook 3 lasagna noodles in 1–2 quarts of boiling water. **Stir** gently until water boils again. **Cook** according to package, about 7–10 minutes. **Drain.**

Spray baking dish with cooking spray

Spread thin layer of pasta sauce on bottom of prepared pan. **Cover** sauce with 1 layer of lasagna noodles, half of the cottage cheese, half of the shredded Mozzarella.

Add 2 tablespoons parsley to the tomato sauce. **Cover** with pasta sauce.

Top with lasagna noodles.

Pour remaining pasta sauce on top. Then **top** with mozzarella.

Cover and seal with aluminium foil. **Refrigerate** overnight.

Preheat oven to 375°F.

Bake on cookie sheet for 25 minutes.

Remove foil and sprinkle with Parmesan cheese.

Bake uncovered for 10 minutes

Set about 10 minutes before serving.

*Prep time **15–20 minutes**   Cook time **35 Minute***

♡ One day before: Cook lasagna noodles and put all ingredients in baking dish. Cover with aluminium foil and refrigerate.

♡ One hour before: Take lasagna out of the refrigerator. Preheat oven.

♡ 45 minutes before: Put lasagna in oven.

♡ 10 minutes before: Take lasagna out of oven. Add Parmesan. Shut off oven and put garlic bread in oven.

ITALIAN SALAD

Pour greens into a salad bowl.

Top with croutons.

Just before serving, **mix** Italian dressing with greens.

GARLIC BREAD

Heat in oven according to package directions.

Remove from oven.

Slice bread into thick slices.

Prep time **5 minutes**

DARK CHOCOLATE ICE CREAM

Serve dark chocolate ice cream in bowls.

Woman Seeking Man: Looking for a man who makes me laugh, enjoys candlelit dinners, walks on the beach and chats in front of the fireside while drinking wine. We don't have to have a fairy-tale romance and live happily ever after like Cinderella and Prince Charming. We could be more like Hollywood romances, couples not bound by anything so conventional as marriage or long-term domestic arrangements. If you remotely meet these criteria, call 1 900 XOXOXOX.

Luke answered this ad, invited Gweneth over for this Italian dinner. They were quickly on their way to a meaningful short-term intimate relationship sparked with great chemistry.

Penne for Your Breakfast Thoughts

1 Do you like to read the paper over breakfast?

2 Are you a morning person?

3 Do you like to exercise in the morning?

4 Do you enjoy a large or light breakfast?

5 Could you fall in love with me?

6 Shall we get together next weekend?

Spring Fling

"There is no season such delight can bring,

as summer, autumn, winter and the spring."

William Browne

When winter turns to spring and your fancy turns to thoughts of mini-skirts, bikinis, tank tops, short shorts, suntans, bleached-blonde hair, convertibles and love; serve one of these dinners. A bouquet of daffodils makes a perfect centrepiece for this fling. Several recipes with chicken breasts have been included because they are on most women's diets.

CHICKEN BREASTS IN SOUR CREAM, RISOTTO, FRESH GARDEN SALAD, RHUBARB STRAWBERRY PIE, TOPPED WITH ICE CREAM AND CHABLIS, CHARDONNAY OR PINOT NOIR

SHOPPING LIST

Produce
2 cups fresh sliced mushrooms

Grocery
1 can mushroom soup

Meat
4 boneless skinless chicken breasts

Dairy
8 ounces sour cream

Liquor
1 cup white wine or cooking sherry for cooking

chablis, chardonnay or pinot noir or gin and tonic to drink

CHICKEN BREASTS IN SOUR CREAM (opposite)

Pour a glass of wine for the cook.

Preheat oven to 350°F.

Place chicken breasts in a 2-1 quart casserole.

Combine mushroom soup, wine and mushrooms.

Pour over chicken.

Bake 45 minutes.

Add sour cream, mix thoroughly and bake an additional 15 minutes.

Serve over risotto (see page 44).

Prep time **15 minutes**   *Cook time* **60 Minutes**

♡ One hour + 15 minutes before: Prepare chicken breasts without sour cream.

♡ One hour before: Bake chicken. Make risotto, turn off burner and cover.

♡ 15 minutes before: Add sour cream and bake 15 minutes more.

♡ Bake rhubarb pie while eating dinner.

"Chicken is for the cook

what canvas is for the painter."

Jean-Anthelme Brillat-Savarin

SHOPPING LIST

Grocery
1 package of risotto rice

RISOTTO (above)

Cook according to package directions.

Scoop risotto onto dinner plates and top with chicken breasts in sour cream.

Prep time **1 minute**

"Risotto is the ultimate comfort food."

Joyce Goldstein

SHOPPING LIST

Frozen Desserts
1 frozen rhubarb or strawberry rhubarb pie
1 pint vanilla ice cream

RHUBARB PIE AND VANILLA ICE CREAM (below)

Bake pie according to directions.

Scoop pie onto plates or bowl and top with ice cream.

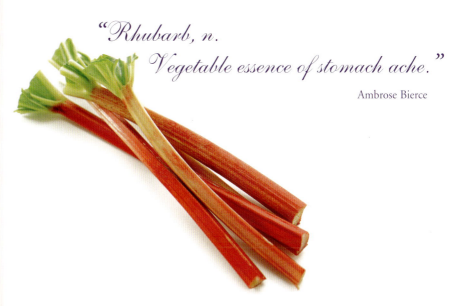

"Rhubarb, n.
Vegetable essence of stomach ache."

Ambrose Bierce

RHUBARB PIE AND VANILLA ICE CREAM
(recipe on page 45)

*"The first rhubarb of the season
    is to the digestive tract of winter-logged inner man
    what a good hot bath with plenty of healing soap
    is to the outer after a bout with plough and harrow.
Even the tongue and teeth
    have a scrubbed feeling after a dish of early rhubarb."*

Della Lutes

Lately Phil's luck has been so bad that he is considering moving to a cabin in the woods, cooking and heating with chopped wood and hunting and fishing for food. Then he meets Amy on a blind date. She invites herself to his place, suggesting she was coming for a good time. Phil fixes this dinner for Amy and the unbelievable happens: she extols that she "will have sex for a lot of good food".

ASPARAGUS RICE (recipe on page 47)

ASPARAGUS RICE, LEMON CHICKEN KABOBS, RASPBERRY YOGURT WITH CHOCOLATE SAUCE AND CHENIN BLANC OR CHAMPAGNE

When life gives you lemons, make marinade. Lemon chicken breast kabobs are finger-licking good. This dinner will have your date believing you are the Leonardo da Vinci of culinary arts. You could purchase lemon-marinated chicken breasts or make this recipe.

Asparagus is a food that looks sexual and is supposed to improve or aid sex. It is also a sex vitamin as it contains vitamin E, potassium, phosphorous and calcium.

ASPARAGUS RICE (opposite)

Cook rice according to package directions.

Add asparagus 3–5 minutes before rice is cooked.

Turn off rice.

Add butter, salt and pepper.

Sprinkle with chopped parsley.

Pour rice into a bowl just before serving.

LEMON CHICKEN KABOBS
(recipe on page 49)

SHOPPING LIST

Produce
2 tablespoons fresh lemon juice

1 tablespoon parsley, chopped

1 clove garlic, minced, or
1 teaspoon minced garlic

¹/₄ teaspoon fresh marjoram or
¹/₄ teaspoon dried marjoram

¹/₂ teaspoon fresh thyme,
oregano and basil leaves

1 cup whole mushrooms

Grocery
¹/₂ cup vegetable oil

1¹/₂ teaspoons red wine vinegar

¹/₃ teaspoon salt

¹/₈ teaspoon black pepper,
freshly ground

Meat
4 boneless, skinless chicken
breasts

Liquor
chenin blanc or champagne
to drink

Miscellaneous
4 x 10" bamboo skewers,
soaked in water

SHOPPING LIST

Frozen Desserts
raspberry frozen yogurt
chocolate sauce

LEMON CHICKEN KABOBS (opposite)

Pour a glass of wine.

Prepare marinade by combining oil, lemon juice, vinegar, parsley, garlic, salt, herbs and pepper in a glass bowl.

Cut chicken into chunks.

Add chunks of chicken and mushrooms to marinade.

Stir to coat.

Cover.

Marinate for 4 hours or overnight in refrigerator.

Drain off marinade.

Start **grill**.

Fill 4–6 skewers with chunks of chicken, alternating with mushrooms.

Grill kebabs 8–10 minutes over medium-high heat, turning once.

Prep time **15 minutes**   *Cook time* **8–10 minutes**

♡ One day before: Prepare marinade, cut up chicken and combine, add mushroom. Soak skewers in water.

♡ 30–60 minutes before: Put chicken and mushrooms on skewers. Cook rice with asparagus; turn off burner, but leave lid on.

♡ 15 minutes before: Grill kebabs. Reheat rice just before serving.

♡ After dinner: Take yogurt from freezer. Heat chocolate sauce.

RASPBERRY YOGURT WITH CHOCOLATE SAUCE

Heat chocolate sauce in a small saucepan while scooping frozen yogurt into bowls.

CHICKEN BREASTS AND ARTICHOKES
(recipe on page 51)

Chicken Breasts and Artichokes, Saffron Rice, Greens with Raspberry Viniagrette

Produce
1 teaspoon chopped parsley

Grocery
4 marinated artichoke hearts, chopped and drained
$1/2$ cup black olives, chopped, and drained
oil for greasing
1 cup breadcrumbs

Dairy
$3/4$ cup Monterey Jack cheese, grated
3 tablespoons butter

Meat
2 skinned boneless chicken breasts

Liquor
$1/2$ cup white wine for cooking
chardonnay to drink

CHICKEN BREASTS AND ARTICHOKES (opposite)

Food, food, food – these three words are as important in developing a relationship as *location, location, location* is when purchasing real estate. At first you talk about it, then prepare it and then share it. Your kitchen is a place where creations come to life.

Pour a glass of wine.

Slice chicken lengthwise to make a pocket.

Mix artichokes, $1/3$ cup olives and cheese.

Stuff artichoke mixture into breasts and place in lightly oiled baking dish.

Refrigerate overnight. Take chicken out of refrigerator 30 minutes before baking. Before baking, **preheat** oven to 350°F.

Bake 20 minutes.

Melt butter in saucepan while breasts are baking.

Add parsley and wine, simmer on low heat and keep warm.

Pour wine mixture over chicken and sprinkle breadcrumbs and remaining olives over chicken.

Bake chicken for another 10 minutes.

Serve chicken breasts on platter.

Prep time **15 minutes**   *Cook time* **30 minutes**

♡ One day before: Prepare chicken and place in baking dish. Cover. Refrigerate.

♡ One hour before: Take chicken out of refrigerator.

♡ 30 minutes before: Bake chicken. Make salads.

♡ 15 minutes before: Cook rice, then turn off burner and leave lid on.

♡ After dinner: Prepare desserts and serve.

SAFFRON RICE AND GREENS WITH VINAIGRETTE
(recipe on page 53)

SAFFRON RICE (opposite)

Cook rice according to package directions.

Serve rice in bowl.

GREENS WITH VINIAGRETTE (opposite)

Place greens on each salad plate.

Top with raisins and sunflower seeds.

Drizzle each salad with vinaigrette.

*Prep time **5 minutes***

Amanda has been having a great time dating in LA, going to gallery openings and hanging out in martini and sushi bars. While all of the guys are great fun, she hasn't found her soul mate, someone who passionately touches her soul. At 30, she meets Greg in the wine section of the grocery store. Both were trying to find the perfect wine for seafood dinners. After a lengthy discussion of white vs. red wine with seafood, they both pick red. They nearly collide in the video section where they again converse about movies and both decide on recent releases. Their last encounter is in the fresh flower section. There, Greg invites Amanda to a baseball game and to his place for dinner afterwards. They both love baseball and it was a double header. The dinner was proof beyond a reasonable doubt that Greg was Amanda's true soul mate.

Warm days, cool nights,

Eating dinner at midnight.

Wake up tomorrow,

Refreshed and bright,

Because you have just spent an evening that was out of sight.

The perfect day, the perfect night,

Sitting in front of candlelight,

The dinner you served was just right,

You know she won't put up a fight.

The wine hits the spot,

The meal was great,

This has been the perfect date.

Brett Hall

SHRIMP WITH ALMOND RICE PILAF, GREENS WITH BALSAMIC VINAIGRETTE
SPARKLING CHAMPAGNE OR CHARDONNAY AND
CHERRY ICE CREAM WITH HOT CHOCOLATE SAUCE

Bold Flavors, Big Impressions, The Secret is in the Spices!

This dinner will have your date believing you are "king of the world".

Jill completes another cardiac Monday-the day most on-the-job heart attacks occur. She is to have dinner at Kent's house that evening. At 4:00pm she attempts to call him to cancel as she is tired to the bone and a hot bath at her place sounds more appealing. Jill calls his office, cell and home phones, only reaching his voice mail. She has no choice but to go to Kent's place at the agreed upon time, hoping he hasn't started dinner. He greets her with a Rum and Coke. Before she can tell him about her change of plans, she smells the shrimp cooking. She decides to stay for dinner, but to leave as soon as it is over. After a few glasses of wine and this mouth-watering dinner, she forgets why *home alone* is so attractive. Kent suggests that Jill take a hot shower and put on his sweats while he cleans up the kitchen and fixes dessert. Jill kisses Kent on the cheek and says, "By the way, would telling you now that I would like to stay all night be enough of a warning?" After nearly choking on his drink, Kent splutters that her warning was definitely sufficient.

SHOPPING LIST

Produce
4 teaspoons minced garlic

1 tablespoon fresh lemon juice

Grocery
4 ounces slivered almonds, toasted

1 cup canned chicken broth

1 cup instant rice

1 teaspoon paprika

Dairy
$^{1}/_{4}$ cup butter

Seafood
1 pound fresh shrimp, peeled and deveined

Frozen Foods
1 cup frozen peas

Liquor
chilled champagne or chardonnay for drinking

rum and coke both regular and diet

SHRIMP WITH ALMOND RICE PILAF (opposite)

Pour a glass of wine.

Peel and **devein** shrimp the day before. **Remove** tails.

Place almonds on cookie sheet and toast in 300°F oven for 6–8 minutes. (This can be done several days before and the almonds stored in a sealed container.)

Bring chicken broth to boil in a medium-sized, heavy based saucepan.

Stir in rice; cover and remove from heat and let stand until liquid is absorbed (about 5 minutes).

Stir in peas and almonds.

Melt butter in medium frying-pan over medium heat. Add garlic, lemon juice and paprika and cook until garlic is golden, stirring occasionally (for about 2 minutes). Caution: garlic can easily burn.

Add uncooked shrimp and cook until opaque, stirring constantly (for about 4 minutes).

Stir in rice mixture and cook until heated through, stirring constantly (for about 2 more minutes).

Prep time **15 minutes**   *Cook time* **20 minutes**

♡ One day before: Toast almonds. If shrimp haven't been peeled and deveined, do it the day before.

♡ 20 minutes before: Cook shrimp.

♡ 15 minutes before: Make salads.

♡ After dinner: Serve ice cream.

SHRIMP WITH ALMOND RICE PILAF

(recipe on page 56)

SHOPPING LIST

Produce
1 bag salad greens

Grocery
croutons
balsamic vinaigrette

GREENS WITH BALSAMIC VINAIGRETTE (below)

Arrange greens on salad plates.

Top with croutons.

Drizzle vinaigrette over salads.

*Prep time **5 minutes***

SHOPPING LIST

Frozen Desserts
cherry ice cream
chocolate sauce, warmed

CHERRY ICE CREAM WITH HOT CHOCOLATE SAUCE

After sharing a bowl of ice cream, your date will be asking, "Can I stay over tonight?" Your response, "Of all of the up-front women I know, you are the up-frontest." And, "Yes."

GREENS WITH BALSAMIC VINAIGRETTE
(recipe on page 58)

GRILLED PEANUT AND GARLIC CHICKEN, SLICED TOMATO, AND POTATO SALAD (recipe on page 60)

Guys and Grills

Fire up the barbecue so you can cook outdoors. Cook chicken breasts, hamburgers, sausages or hot dogs. Slice a fresh tomato. Buy potato salad from the deli. Chardonnay with chicken, or beer with the sausages, hot dogs or hamburgers: the perfect summertime meal.

While grocery shopping, buy fresh flowers. You might even splurge and get a couple of bouquets. Your florist will make recommendations so your home looks inviting and intimate and not like the rose bowl parade.

"After eating chocolate you feel godlike,
as though you can conquer enemies,
lead armies, entice lovers."

Emily Luchetti

GRILLED PEANUT AND GARLIC CHICKEN, SLICED TOMATO, POTATO SALAD AND CHARDONNAY (photograph on page 59)

Pour a glass of wine.

Combine chicken and Asian peanut sauce in medium bowl; coat chicken with sauce.

Place coated chicken in a plastic bag then,

Refrigerate for at least 2 hours or overnight.

Heat oiled barbecue grill.

Grill chicken 7–8 minutes on each side, turning once.

Sprinkle chicken with cilantro after placing on platter.

Serve with sliced tomato and potato salad.

*Prep time **2¹/₂ hours**   Cook time **15 minutes***

♡ One day before: Pour sauce over chicken breasts; refrigerate in ziplock or covered container overnight

♡ 30 minutes before: Heat barbecue and grill chicken breasts. Slice tomato. Pour potato salad into a serving bowl

GRILLED SAUSAGES, SLICED TOMATO, POTATO SALAD AND
COLD BEER (recipe on page 61)

SHOPPING LIST

Produce
1 tomato, sliced for side dish

Grocery
vegetable oil
black pepper (optional)

Meat
4 fully cooked sausages

Deli
1 pint potato salad

Miscellaneous
1 pastry brush

Liquor
beer to drink

GRILLED SAUSAGES, SLICED TOMATO, POTATO SALAD AND COLD BEER (above)

Pour a beer into a chilled mug.

Preheat grill.

Oil barbecue grill rack using a pastry brush or paper towel.

Grill sausages, turning frequently, until browned and heated through.

Season with pepper, if desired.

Serve with sliced tomato and potato salad.

Prep time **3 minutes**   *Cook time* **10–12 minutes**

♡ 30 minutes before: Heat grill.

♡ 15 minutes before: Oil barbecue grill. Put sausages on grill.
Slice tomato. Pour potato salad into serving bowl.

> *"The noblest of all dogs is the hotdog; It feeds the hand that bites it."*
>
> Laurence J. Peter

SHOPPING LIST

Produce

$^1/_2$ onion, chopped

1 tomato, chopped

1 extra tomato, sliced,
for side dish

Grocery

ketchup

mustard

chopped pickled peppers

pickle relish

pickle spears

Meat

4 Vienna Beef hot dogs

Bakery

4 hotdog buns

Deli

1 pint potato salad

Liquor

beer to drink

CHICAGO-STYLE HOT DOGS, SLICED TOMATO, POTATO SALAD AND COLD BEER

*Delicious, fool proof, mouth-watering and
nutrition-free hot dogs.*

Most women won't readily admit their passion for hot dogs. While at the show, at the airport or while attending a baseball game, women will be first in the hot dog line.

Pour a cold beer.

Cut hot dog buns in half (but not all the way through).

Preheat barbecue grill. **Grill** hot dogs.

Place hot dogs in hot dog buns. **Top** with ketchup, mustard, peppers, relish and onion.

Serve with pickle spears, sliced tomato and potato salad.

Prep time **5 minutes**   *Cook time* **5–10 minutes**

♡ One day before: Chop onion and peppers, put in a baggie and store in refrigerator.

♡ 15 minutes before: Heat barbecue grill and put hot dogs on grill when it gets hot. Slice tomato. Pour potato salad into serving bowl.

HAMBURGER (recipe on page 64)

Hamburger was unanimously voted into America's Culinary Hall of Fame. You can shock your date with the disappointing information that the hamburger did not originate in America. Germany, though not Hamburg, gets the credit. There are numerous theories about how the hamburger landed on a bun, possibly at a New York delicatessen; another that it was first served with a bun at the St. Louis Fair.

However the hamburger and bun became a couple, the hamburger has taken over the country.

To make hamburgers for a date, you can add interesting ingredients to make this classic even more special.

HAMBURGERS, SLICED TOMATOES AND ONIONS, HOME-FRIED POTATOES AND BEER

SHOPPING LIST

Produce
2–3 tablespoons finely grated onion
1 tomato, sliced for side dish

Grocery
freshly ground black pepper
salt

Dairy
1 tablespoon heavy cream

Bakery
1 package hamburger buns, buttered or 1 packet of English muffins

Meat
2 pounds top quality chopped round or chuck steak

Liquor
beer to drink

SHOPPING LIST

Grocery
2 tablespoons vegetable oil
salt and pepper

Frozen Vegetable Section
1 package of home fries or hash browns

HAMBURGER (photograph on page 63)

No ketchup or condiments will be needed for this creamy, oniony flavor that runs through the meat.

Spread chopped round or chuck steak on a chopping board.

Top with grated onion.

Combine pepper with heavy cream and pour over onions. Using your hands, **mix** thoroughly.

Form into patties, about 6–8 ounces each.

Grill or **cook** in a heavy skillet over a fairly high heat.

Cook about 4–5 minutes per side.

Sprinkle with salt and serve on buns.

Serve with sliced tomato.

Prep time **10 minutes**   *Cook time* **10 minutes**

♡ One hour before: Mix chopped round or chuck steak with onions, cream and pepper. Form patties.

♡ 30 minutes before: Fry potatoes. Slice tomato.

♡ 10 minutes before: Grill or cook hamburgers.

HOME-FRIED POTATOES (opposite)

Cook according to package directions.

Bob and Kelly go to Bob's favorite restaurant on their first date. Bob chooses a table in a remote corner away from the waiter, but the night is a total disaster. Both see several partners from former relationships, as well as several business acquaintances, all stopping by their table. While the food is great, the conversation is difficult due to constant interruptions. Bob wants to get to know Kelly and assumes she wants the same, so he invites her to his place for grilled hamburgers. Casual dining and clever conversation seduce her. Soon they are *counting the ceiling fan revolutions per minute in his bedroom.*

Chill While You Grill

After an afternoon of roller-blading, invite your date to your place for a grilled dinner served on the deck. When there is smoke, there is flavor! For the simplest grilled dinner ever, put it in a foil bag, start the grill and lie back in your hammock or lawn chairs while dinner is cooking. Eat dinner by candlelight or moonlight. This evening will be *as good as it gets.*

SHOPPING LIST

Produce

¹/₂ large sweet onion, sliced

4 new potatoes, sliced

4 mushrooms, sliced

¹/₂ large red pepper, sliced

Grocery

olive oil cooking spray

¹/₂ teaspoon garlic powder

¹/₂ teaspoon salt-free lemon pepper

¹/₂ teaspoon salt

¹/₂ teaspoon cracked pepper

¹/₂ teaspoon Worcestershire sauce

¹/₂ teaspoon balsamic vinegar

¹/₂ tablespoon olive oil

Meat

2 chicken breasts

Miscellaneous

*1 foil bag, regular size, or two
pieces of 10 x 12 inches foil*

oven mitts

Liquor

*sauvignon blanc or chenin blanc
to drink*

SHOPPING LIST

Grocery

*1 box couscous, plain or any
flavor like chicken*

CHICKEN IN A BAG (opposite)

Pour a glass of wine.

Heat grill.

Open foil bag.

Spray foil with cooking spray.

Build packets with onion slices on bottom, then potatoes, chicken, mushrooms and top with red pepper.

Sprinkle liberally with spices, salt, pepper, Worcestershire sauce and balsamic vinegar.

Drizzle olive oil on top.

Fold and seal edges of foil bag.

Grill 1 hour on medium-low, indirect heat.

Cut open foil bag with a sharp knife (wear oven mitts).

Fold back top of foil bag, allowing steam to escape.

Serve on platter.

Prep time **10 minutes**   *Cook time* **1 hour**

♡ 14 Days before: Make Stoli Dole and refrigerate.

♡ 70 minutes before: Put together chicken in a bag.

♡ 1 hour before: Grill chicken in a bag.

♡ 15 minutes before: Make couscous. Cover when done.

COUSCOUS (opposite)

Cook according to package directions.

SHOPPING LIST

Produce
1 fresh pineapple

Liquor
Stoli vodka

STOLI DOLE

Pour vodka into a plastic container with cubed fresh pineapple. **Seal** and **refrigerate** for 14 days.

Serve straight up or over ice.

Prep time **14 days**

Randy escapes the high-stress corporate life in San Francisco, moves to an island and lives in a beach house. He works as a bartender, entertaining beautiful natives and tourists with his imitation of Tom Cruise in *Cocktail*. There he meets Ellen, a writer, who is on vacation for the first time in three years. While they are physically attracted to one another, their contrasting lifestyles, current professions and political affiliations constantly clash. She is a raging liberal and he a compassionate conservative. After spending more time together, it appears their relationship will end when her vacation is over. On their last night together, Randy serves one of his special pineapple drinks and grills this dinner in a bag. They sit on the beach and talk for hours, finally finding that their commonalties exceed their differences. They have been shacking up together ever since.

Hot August Nights

Maybe it's all that exposed skin or the hot, humid nights; whatever the reason, in the summertime it is time to turn up the heat on summer romance. The summertime fireworks can go off in your bedroom.

If you are feeling beachy and cannot make it to the sea or lake, head for the back porch with your lover and enjoy cool drinks on a hot summer night. Cool summer drinks are the crisper white wines, like sauvignon blanc. The American standard is cold beer. If you prefer mixed drinks, gin or vodka with tonic, and rum drinks are good. The easiest rum drink is with Coke. Peach Fuzz is a blender drink that tastes great and is so divine that several blenders later your evening will be a scene from *9¹/2 Weeks*.

COUSCOUS SALAD (recipe on page 69)

Couscous Salad or Mozzarella Salad, Flat Bread, Sauvignon Blanc and Angel Food Cake Topped with Strawberry shortcake ice cream

Couscous Salad (opposite)

Pour a glass of wine.

Slice tomatoes in half.

Bring chicken broth to boil in a medium saucepan.

Add couscous, remove from heat and cover; let stand for 5 minutes. **Transfer** to a large bowl.

Fluff couscous with a fork and cool completely. **Mix** in all ingredients.

Season with salt and pepper.

Prep time **10 minutes**   *Cook time* **2 minutes**

♡ 30 minutes before: Wash strawberries or blueberries; drain.

♡ 10 minutes before: Make couscous salad.

♡ 10 minutes before serving dessert: Take ice cream out of freezer and strawberries from refrigerator. Slice cake and top with ice cream and fresh strawberries or blueberries.

Mozzarella Salad

Mix tomato, cheese and bread.

Whisk oil and vinegar together with salt, pepper and red hot pepper.

Pour over tomato mixture.

Serve on plates.

Prep time **10 minutes**

> *"The most dangerous food a man can eat is wedding cake."*
>
> American proverb

SHOPPING LIST

Produce
2 cups fresh strawberries

Bakery
1 angel food cake

Frozen Desserts
1 pint strawberry ice cream or vanilla ice cream and fresh strawberries

ANGEL FOOD CAKE TOPPED WITH STRAWBERRY ICE CREAM (opposite)

Slice angel food cake.

Put slices on salad or dessert plates.

Put a scoop of ice cream on each slice.

Top with fresh strawberries.

Prep time **10 minutes**

If you can't stand the heat ... get in the kitchen and make something cool. You won't sweat while making a super deli sandwich using good quality breads, making cucumbers in sour cream, preparing fresh berries, and possibly opening a bag of chips.

Play 'Love Shack' by the B-52s (Cosmic Thing) and celebrate a flavor-fest of deli sandwiches, fresh fruit and a cold drink.

You could pick up sandwiches, cucumbers in sour cream and fresh fruit from the deli. Or you can make the sandwiches using these recipes.

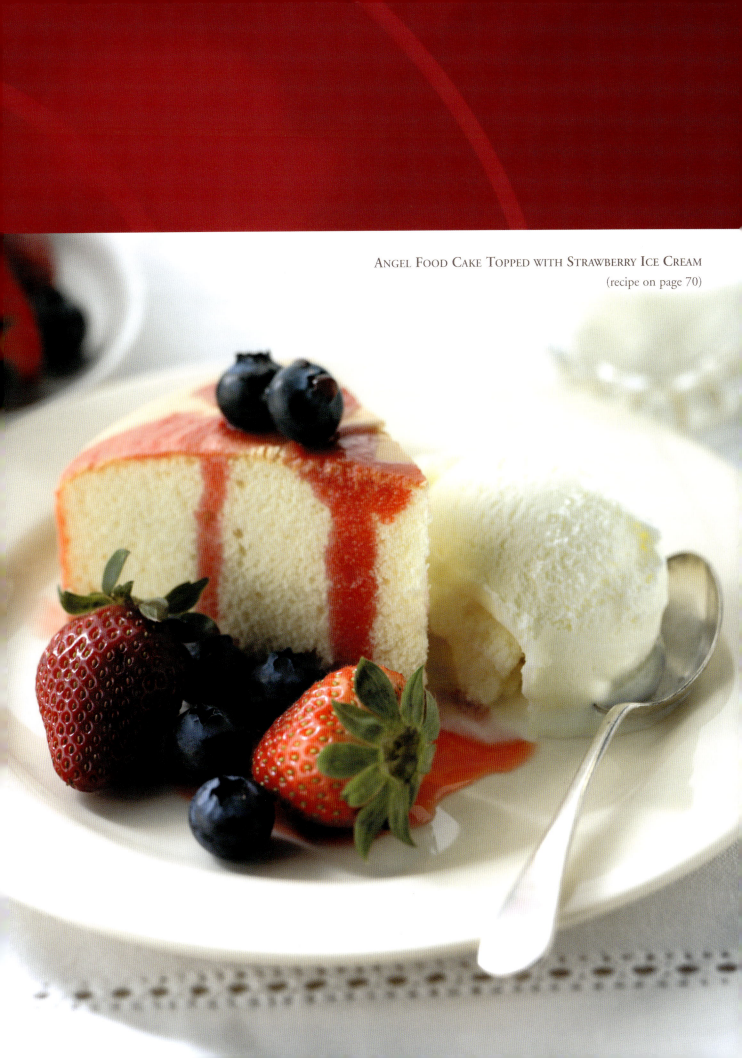

ANGEL FOOD CAKE TOPPED WITH STRAWBERRY ICE CREAM

(recipe on page 70)

SHOPPING LIST

Bakery
4 slices of pumpernickel or wholewheat bread

Deli
8 ounces sliced deli roast beef

2 slices of Swiss or cheddar cheese or provolone

pickle spears, sweet or dill

Grocery
mayonnaise

small jars of mustard

Liquor
chardonnay to drink

BEEF SANDWICH (opposite)

A fresh sandwich that is a gastronomical delight. You could substitute turkey or ham for the beef.

Pour a rum and Coke.

On a slice of bread, **arrange** roast beef, 4 ounces on each slice.

Top with cheese and remaining slice of bread.

To serve, cut each sandwich in half and place on plate.

Put pickle spears on both sides of sandwich.

Put mayonnaise in small bowl with a small knife.

Put small knives in mustards.

Prep time **5 minutes**

♡ 45 minutes before: Make cucumbers and sour cream.

♡ 15 minutes before: Wash berries.

♡ 5 minutes before: Make sandwiches.

SHOPPING LIST

Grocery
7 ounces chunk white albacore tuna, drained

$1/4$ cup raisins

$1/4$ cup pecan pieces

$1/4$ cup mayonnaise

Bakery
4 slices whole wheat bread

TUNA, RAISIN AND PECAN SANDWICH

Mix all ingredients and spread on bread.

Cut sandwiches in half and serve.

Prep time **10 minutes**

♡ One hour before: Make tuna salad, leaving out pecans. Store in refrigerator, covered.

♡ 45 minutes before: Make cucumber and sour cream.

♡ 15 minutes before: Wash berries.

♡ 10 minutes before: Make sandwiches.

"*You are a buff guy who's been beefing up to look good for a beefcake calendar . . . so what's your beef?!*"

Sharon Tyler Herbst

BEEF SANDWICH (recipe on page 72)

Produce
4 lettuce leaves
8 tomato slices

Grocery
salt and pepper
$^1/_4$ cup light mayonnaise

Bakery
8 slices wholewheat bread,
toasted

Meat
8 slices bacon

BLT (opposite)

When it is BLT season, serve your date this timeless sandwich and savor America's terrific summer sandwich. The combination of crisp bacon, fresh tomatoes, lettuce and fresh bread is deliciously appealing.

Pour a gin and tonic or a beer.

Microwave cooked bacon so heated through and crisp (about 1 minute).

Use a paper towel to absorb excess grease.

Toast bread.

Lightly **sprinkle** salt and pepper on tomato slices.

Layer each of 4 bread slices with 1 tablespoon mayonnaise, 1 lettuce leaf, 2 tomato slices and 2 pieces of bacon.

Top with remaining bread slices.

Slice each sandwich in half.

Prep time **10 minutes**   *Cook time* **1 minute**

♡ 45 minutes before: Make cucumber and sour cream.

♡ 15 minutes before: Make berries.

♡ 5 minutes before: Make BLTs.

SHOPPING LIST

Produce
4 cucumbers, peeled and sliced
$^1/_2$ medium onion, chopped

Grocery
1 teaspoon cider vinegar
salt and pepper

Dairy
$^1/_2$–1 cup sour cream

Miscellaneous
paper towels

CUCUMBERS AND SOUR CREAM

Sprinkle salt on sliced cucumbers and refrigerate for 30 minutes.

Pat cucumbers with paper towels to absorb moisture.

Add chopped onion.

Mix sour cream, vinegar, salt and pepper.

Drain cucumber and onion; add sour cream mixture.

Serve in a bowl.

Prep time **45 minutes**

BLT (recipe on page 74)

SHOPPING LIST

Produce
1 cup fresh strawberries, sliced
1 cup fresh blueberries
1 cup fresh raspberries

FRESH BERRIES

Any combination of berries, is a great summer treat.

Toss berries with sugar.

Serve in a bowl.

Prep time 5 minutes

> *"Forget the cheap white wine, go for the beef and gin!"*
>
> Julia Child

GIN OR VODKA AND TONIC

Pour 1 shot of vodka or gin over ice.

Fill glass with tonic.

Garnish with 1 slice of lime.

PEACH FUZZ

This drink is so smooth and refreshing, you will drink 3–4 blenders of it.

Remove stone from 1 peach.

Put 1 peach in blender along with 1 can of frozen lemonade.

Fill empty can with vodka and pour vodka into blender.

Fill blender three-quarters full with ice.

Blend until drink is smooth and free of ice chunks.

RUM AND COKE

Pour 1 shot of rum over ice.

Fill glass with Coke or diet Coke.

Garnish with 1 slice of lime.

Chad hasn't been dating for a while as his relationships end for no apparent reason. To better understand women, he watches fourteen movies for the female soul, a 30-minute infomercial about a device that gets rid of wrinkles and five 'Golden Girls' re-runs. He learns several things: if you take all of the good parts from all of the men in those movies, you can't come up with one whole man. He also learns that women actually buy gizmos to get rid of wrinkles. When he starts to have a "fatal attraction" for Betty White, he decides it is time to go for a walk. He takes his dog, Barney, to the park, hoping to meet a woman who isn't a member of the geriatric set, convince her he has redeeming qualities and to tell her he finds wrinkles fetching. There he runs into Allison who recently moved into his apartment building. Both are attracted to one another but haven't found a way to expand parking-lot greetings to a real conversation. Allison immediately makes friends with Chad's dog and then with Chad. They sit on a park bench and talk for hours. Chad invites Allison to his place for a sandwich and beer. After three months, they are still together without turning the television on once.

Note: When you walk with a dog rather than alone, more strangers will approach your dog and will then start talking with you. Even if you do not become friends with the strangers, your dog will have a larger circle of acquaintances.

Autumn Intermezzo

"The best of times is now.
What's left of summer? But a faded rose?
The best of times is now."

Jerry Herman

On a crisp fall afternoon, start a fire in your indoor or outdoor fireplace, smell the fall and shove the sun back up into the sky to give you one more day of sunshine. On that glorious afternoon, invite someone special for a feast of fall flavors. Fall is a time to enjoy the abundance of good food that has just been harvested.

For those of you dreading the end of the World Series and a winter without baseball, watch a baseball movie with a romantic storyline. Don't forget that you can pause the movie at any time. This meal, ambience and movie should get you to all bases, and possibly the upper deck.

Gourds, pumpkins and squash can be hollowed out and used as vases for autumn flowers. They have rich and warm colors that contrast the greens and oranges of the squash and pumpkins. Large round scented candles can be set in the middle of your autumn arrangement or in a pumpkin or squash or in the middle of a bowl of apples.

SHOPPING LIST

Produce
2 teaspoons minced garlic

Grocery
4 tablespoons Worcestershire sauce

Meat
2 pork chops (chops that are 1 inch thick)

Liquor
pinot noir or semillon and cognac to drink

SHOPPING LIST

Produce
2 sweet potatoes

Grocery
salt, pepper, lemon pepper, brown sugar and cinnamon

Dairy
butter

Experience this provocative porcine dinner paired with fall fruits and vegetables along with sultry wine.

GRILLED PORK CHOPS – PORK THE ONE YOU LOVE (opposite)

Pour a glass of wine.

Marinate chops in Worcestershire sauce and garlic for two hours.

Grill on both sides until cooked so there is no pink in the middle.

*Prep time **2 hours**   Cook time **10 minutes***

♡ Two hours before: Marinate chops in glass container, cover and refrigerate. Wash potatoes.

♡ One hour before: Bake sweet potatoes. Prepare apples for baking.

♡ 30 minutes before: Heat grill.

♡ 15 minutes before: Grill chops. Put apples in oven and set timer for 40 minutes.

BAKED SWEET POTATO

Preheat oven to 350°F

Bake sweet potato at 350°F for an hour.

Cut sweet potato with a sharp knife before serving.

Sweet potatoes can be topped with butter and salt and pepper; butter and lemon pepper; or butter with brown sugar and cinnamon.

*Cook time **20 minutes to 1 hour***

"*Cognac ... a sense of amusement, charm, excitement,*
all combined into the purest of pleasure."
Roy Andries de Groot

GRILLED PORK CHOPS (recipe on page 78)

SHOPPING LIST

Produce
2 crisp apples such as Granny Smith

Grocery
4 tablespoons brown sugar
$^1/_4$ teaspoon ground cinnamon
2 tablespoons walnuts
2 teaspoons quick oatmeal

Dairy
1 tablespoon butter

Frozen Desserts
cinnamon or vanilla ice cream

BAKED APPLES WITH CINNAMON ICE CREAM (above)

An easier dessert would be to buy frozen apple dumplings, bake according to package directions and top with vanilla ice cream.

Preheat oven to 375°F°.

Slice bottoms off apples and core them.

Generously **butter** a glass baking dish.

Arrange apples upright in dish.

Fill the center of each apple with brown sugar, cinnamon, walnuts, oatmeal and leftover butter.

Bake apples for 30–45 minutes, until soft.

Apples or apple dumplings can be baking while you are eating the pork chops and sweet potatoes. Transfer apples or apple dumplings to individual bowls and top with cinnamon or vanilla ice cream.

Prep time **10 minutes**   *Cook time* **30 minutes**

SHOPPING LIST

Grocery
1 teaspoon dried rosemary
1 teaspoon dried thyme
$1/2$ teaspoon white pepper
1 tablespoon pine nuts

Dairy
1 tablespoon goat cheese

Meat
2 pork chops, 1 inch thick

Liquor
semillon chardonnay blend to drink

STUFFED PORK CHOPS (photograph on page 82)

Combine rosemary, thyme, pepper, nuts and goat cheese.

Cut a slit in each chop.

Stuff each with half of the goat cheese paste.

Heat grill.

Grill chops for 4–5 minutes on each side.

Prep time **15 minutes**   *Cook time* **10 minutes**

♡ One hour before: Mix spices, nuts and goat cheese. Cut pork. Cover both with plastic wrap and refrigerate. Wash potatoes.

♡ 45 minutes before: Spoon cheese mixture into chops. Sauté peaches and turn off.

♡ 30 minutes before: Cook potatoes. Arrange greens on salad plates. Start grill.

♡ 15 minutes before: Grill chops. Top salad with croutons and dressing.

MASHED POTATOES

Quarter potatoes and **put** them in a saucepan; **cover** with cold water.

Bring to **boil** and **cook** until done, about 20–30 minutes.

Use a sharp knife to test for doneness.

Using a potato masher or fork, **mash** potatoes a few times.

Pour potatoes into a serving dish, top with butter and **sprinkle** with salt and pepper.

Prep time **5 minutes**   *Cook time* **20–30 minutes**

STUFFED PORK CHOPS (recipe on page 81)

SHOPPING LIST

Produce
1 bag of salad greens

Grocery
croutons
poppy seed dressing

GREENS WITH POPPY SEED DRESSING (above)

Arrange greens on salad plates, top with croutons and drizzle dressing over the greens.

*Prep time **5 minutes***

SHOPPING LIST

Produce
4 fresh peaches (or canned peaches when fresh are not available)

Grocery
2 tablespoons brown sugar
$1/2$ teaspoon cinnamon

Dairy
2 tablespoons butter
2 tablespoons orange juice

Frozen Desserts
vanilla ice cream

Liquor
late harvest sauvignon blanc
dessert wine to drink

SHOPPING LIST

Liquor
peach brandy

SAUTÉED PEACHES (below)

Melt butter in skillet.

Add brown sugar and cinnamon.

Stir until brown sugar dissolves.

Add orange juice and stir.

Add peaches and sauté until browned and heated through.

Serve peaches over vanilla ice cream.

Prep time **10 minutes**   *Cook time* **10 minutes**

*"An apple is an excellent thing,
until you have tried a peach!"*

George du Maurier

PEACH BRANDY

The easiest dessert of all is serving peach brandy over ice. It is also very good.

SAUTÉED PEACHES (recipe on page 84)

SHOPPING LIST

Produce

3 tablespoons chopped garlic

2 tablespoons grated ginger

3 jalapeño peppers, minced

2 tablespoons fresh lemon juice

Grocery

2 tablespoons olive oil

salt and pepper

Meat

1 boneless pork loin

Miscellaneous

large oven baggie, big enough to hold loin

roasting pan or large pan with oven-safe handle

meat thermometer, if you don't already have one

aluminum foil

Liquor

cabernet sauvignon, shiraz or, better yet, sangiovese (don't buy it from the $5.99 shelf because your woman will know that she doesn't rate the GOOD stuff.)

CUBAN PORK LOIN WITH CHILIES AND GINGER

(photograph on page 86)

Put garlic, ginger, minced jalapeño peppers, lemon juice and olive oil, in a bowl. **Mix** it really well so it becomes a paste.

Spread paste over pork loin, place in baggie.

Seal baggie; **put** it in the refrigerator and marinate overnight.

Turn marinated pork loin before you go to bed.

Turn container again before you go to work. When you get home from work, **pour** yourself a cocktail and turn the loin.

Take loin out of refrigerator 30 minutes before it goes into the oven.

Preheat oven to 350°F.

Freshen up that cocktail – by now you need it.

Put loin in a roasting pan or a big frying-pan.

Spread remaining paste from the baggie over the loin.

Bake loin for 40–60 minutes, depending on the size of the roast.

Insert thermometer at 40 minutes. When thermometer reads 145°F, take loin out of the oven.

Put loin on a cutting board and cover it with foil.

Let it **set** for 20 minutes.

Carve the loin in $^3/4$ inch slices and place two of them artistically on each plate. Lightly salt and pepper each slice.

*Prep time **12 hours**   Cook time **40–60 minutes***

♡ Day before: Make marinade and put loin in oven baggie. Seal and refrigerate. Turn loin before you go to bed.

♡ Before you go to work: Turn loin.

♡ 65 minutes before: Preheat oven. Roast loin.

♡ 30 minutes before: Cook rice. Open wine.

♡ 5 minutes before: Heat beans.

Tips:

1 Mincing the jalapeños – cut the stem off each chili, cut each chili in half, remove seeds, and cut into tiny pieces, about $^1/_{16}$ inch square. When you cut or chop chilies use gloves or put your hand inside a baggie; if you don't, be sure not to rub your eyes before next Tuesday.

2 You don't have to have a juicer to squeeze a lemon – microwave for 30 seconds, roll it on the counter, cut it in half and squeeze. If you are strong, you can get 3 tablespoons of lemon juice from $1–1^1/_2$ lemons. If not, it may take 2 lemons. You can squeeze the lemon juice through your fingers to catch the seeds and pulp.

3 If you bake the pork loin in a frying-pan, be sure the pan has an oven-safe handle.

SHOPPING LIST

Grocery
instant brown rice

SHOPPING LIST

Grocery
1 can black beans

Miscellaneous
slotted spoon

BROWN RICE

Cook according to package directions.

BLACK BEANS

Heat beans in a pan and throw away the can; no sense advertising that you are serving canned food.

Use a slotted spoon to serve the beans, so you won't get black liquid all over your pork.

David has been a widower for a year, eating restaurant takeout every night. Every friend he knows is trying to line him with up with their single sisters, cousins and friends. He reluctantly goes on a few first dates, promising to call each of them. Hopefully they don't sit at home holding their breath waiting for those calls. David decides to take cooking classes so he can make his own dinners as he really misses home-cooked meals. There he learns to cook and meets Molly. For a first date, David prepares this dinner. Later that evening, David remembers the other thing he was missing – intimacy.

SHOPPING LIST

Produce
2 tablespoons fresh rosemary,
keeping a couple of sprigs
for garnish
3 teaspoons minced garlic

Grocery
3 tablespoons olive oil
1 tablespoon balsamic vinegar
1 teaspoon freshly ground
pepper
1 teaspoon salt

Butcher
2 pound pork loin

Liquor
merlot to drink

Miscellaneous
meat thermometer
aluminium foil

ROSEMARY PORK (opposite)

Preheat oven to 350°F.

Grease pan with olive oil.

Cut roast in half lengthwise.

Chop rosemary into a bowl using a knife or scissors.

Add olive oil, garlic, balsamic vinegar, salt and pepper.

Pour sauce over inside of pork.

Bake about 60 minutes or until internal temperature of pork is 170°F.

Remove from oven, cover with foil and let meat set for 20 minutes.

When ready to serve, **cut** thin slices of pork and arrange on a platter.

Pour juices over meat.

Garnish with fresh rosemary sprigs.

Prep time **15 minutes**   *Cook time* **60 minutes**

♡ One day before: Toast walnuts.

♡ 80 minutes before: Bake pork roast. Take mashed potatoes out of freezer.

♡ 25 minutes before: Take pork from oven and cover. Make salad.

♡ 15 minutes before: Prepare potatoes.

♡ 5 minutes before: Slice pork.

ROSEMARY PORK (recipe on page 88)

Produce
*1 tablespoon fresh chives,
chopped*
1 tablespoon butter
2 tablespoons milk
freshly ground black pepper

Frozen Vegetables
*1 package of fresh or frozen
mashed potatoes*

Produce
1 package of greens
1 apple, cored and sliced
1 orange, sectioned

Produce
¹/₂ cup walnuts, toasted
*2 tablespoons walnut or
champagne vinaigrette*

Dairy
*2 tablespoons goat or blue
cheese, crumbled*

MASHED POTATOES WITH CHIVES

Heat mashed potatoes according to package directions and add chives, butter
and freshly ground black pepper.

Prep time **5 minutes**   *Cook time* **20 minutes raw; 5 minutes frozen**

GREENS WITH WALNUT VINAIGRETTE

Toast walnuts on baking tray in 325°F oven. Walnuts should smell toasted
but not burned.

Put greens on plate, top with apple and orange slices.

Sprinkle walnuts and cheese on top.

Drizzle with vinaigrette.

Prep time **10 minutes**

Teriyaki Pork Loin, Fried Rice, Petit Syrah or Red Zinfadel
Pears, Stilton Cheese and Walnuts and Port Wine

Start the grill before she arrives. Pour a glass of wine when she arrives and place the pork loin on the barbecue.

Teriyaki Pork Loin (opposite)

You can purchase a pork loin that has been marinated with teriyaki or make your own marinade using the following recipe. Always cook pork on medium heat. Allow approximately 20 minutes per pound.

Pour a glass of wine.

Combine all ingredients, except tenderloin; mix well.

Place loin in oven bag and pour marinade over loin. **Close** bag and tie securely.

Marinate in refrigerator for 8–24 hours.

Start **barbecue** grill. **Remove** loin from bag.

Place loin on medium-hot grill.

Grill until meat thermometer reaches 175°F. (Approximately 25–30 minutes)

Brush loin occasionally with marinade while grilling.

Prep time 8–24 hours   Cook time 30–60 minutes

♡ Day before: Make marinade. Place loin in a baggie and pour marinade over. Refrigerate.

♡ Two hours before: Take Stilton cheese out of the refrigerator.

♡ One hour before: Take pork out of the refrigerator. Start barbecue grill.

♡ 55 minutes before: Grill meat. When done, place on cutting board and cover with foil.

♡ 30 minutes before: Put cheese on a plate and surround it with sliced pears and walnuts.

♡ 15 Minutes before: Cook rice. When rice is cooked, slice pork.

TERIYAKI PORK LOIN (recipe on page 90)

SHOPPING LIST

Produce
1 package of fried rice

SHOPPING LIST

Produce
2 fresh ripe pears, sliced (or canned pears, drained)

Grocery
1 package of walnuts

Dairy
1 package Stilton cheese, at room temperature

Liquor
port wine to drink

FRIED RICE

Cook rice according to package directions.

PEARS, STILTON CHEESE AND WALNUTS

Take cheese out of refrigerator two hours before serving. Just before serving, **core** and **slice** pears.

If serving canned pears, **drain** in colander. **Slice** pears.

Put cheese in the center of a plate, surround it with sliced pears and walnuts. A small knife is needed to cut the cheese.

Serve with port.

Prep time **10 minutes**

SHOPPING LIST

Produce
garlic cloves
fresh basil
fresh spinach
fresh mushrooms
1 red pepper
1 onion

Grocery
1 can diced tomatoes
1 jar marinated artichokes
3–4 small pizza crusts

Dairy
mozzarella, provolone and
Parmesan cheese

Meat
sausage or pizza sausage
bacon

Liquor
Corona or any special premium
beer to drink

Pizza and Beer Sleepover

While your favorite pizza delivery is #1 on your speed dial and her favorite pizza delivery is #3, and create your own. It will be the best pizza you and your date will ever eat. When inviting her over, jokingly ask if she wants to come over for pizza and sex? And when she says no, respond, "why, don't you like pizza?"

Included are several pizza recipes. You could also buy several small pizza crusts, along with numerous toppings, and really start thinking *outside the box*, creating never-before-tried combinations. You will need olive oil, minced garlic, fresh basil, 1 can of diced tomatoes, marinated artichokes, fresh spinach, fresh mushrooms, red peppers, brown onions, mozzarella, provolone, Parmesan, sausage, bacon, and any of your other favorite toppings. After this evening of tweaking pizza toppings, decide who is the worst pizza maker and that person will have to clean up the kitchen. At the end of the evening, you both will be reprogramming your speed dials, eliminating the pizza deliveries and replacing it with each other's #

For an encore evening, you could make your own crusts, learning new skills like kneading, dough rising and then shaping the dough. Just add the various toppings and pop your creations into the oven.

BEER: It's not just for men anymore. Suggested beers: Corona with lime, Anchor Steam or a micro brewery beer. Always keep a supply of beer glasses in the freezer.

Annette has been dating Michael for about a month. Michael wants a closer relationship but Annette is up-tight in fact tighter than lug nuts on a 1955 Chevy. Their dates include fine dining, theatre and sailing. Michael invites Annette to his place for pizza and beer. She accepts his unpretentious invitation. They drink Corona with lime slices while making pizza. Maybe it was the beer or the relaxed atmosphere of unplanned spontaneity that loosens her up. The author has no advice on what you do with a woman with loose lug nuts, only tight ones.

SHOPPING LIST

Produce

5 teaspoons minced garlic

1/2 medium red onion

2 tablespoons fresh basil, chopped

Grocery

1 tablespoon olive oil

4 sun-dried tomato halves, thinly sliced

Deli

1 pizza crust

1/2 cup Italian fontina cheese, grated

1 cup mozzarella cheese, grated

Seafood

4 ounces medium shrimp, shelled and deveined

SHRIMP AND SUN-DRIED TOMATO PIZZA (above)

Preheat oven to 400°F.

Place pizza crust on baking sheet and brush with oil.

Sprinkle with fontina and mozzarella, leaving 1/2 inch border.

Arrange garlic, onion, chopped basil, shrimp and sun-dried tomatoes over the cheese.

Bake for 10–12 minutes. Cheese should bubble.

Prep time **10 minutes** *Cook time* **10–12 minutes**

Beer for thought: Beauty is in the eye of the beer holder.

SHOPPING LIST

Produce
$1/2$ cup sliced red pepper

$1/4$ yellow onion, sliced thinly

$1/4$ cup mushrooms

Grocery
1 pizza crust

1 can pizza sauce

Meat
1 package Canadian bacon, chopped

Dairy
4 ounces smoked provolone, grated

CANADIAN BACON PIZZA

Heat oven to 400°F.

Spread pizza sauce on the pizza crust.

Add Canadian bacon.

Cover with vegetables.

Sprinkle with grated cheese.

Bake for about 10 minutes or until vegetables have softened and cheese has melted.

If you or your date prefer wine with pizza, a perfect match would be sauvignon blanc, loaded with passionfruit flavors with a touch of citrus zest and a crisp succulent finish. Plant yourself in front of the TV with your lover and pop in a movie.

Prep time **15 minutes**   *Cook time* **10+ minutes**

SHOPPING LIST

Grocery
2.82 ounce jar pesto

6 ounce jar marinated artichoke hearts, drained and chopped

$1/8$ teaspoon black pepper

Deli
12 inch pizza crust, pre-baked

Dairy
$1/2$ cup mozzarella, grated

Meat
20 ounce package Italian-flavored, fully cooked chicken, cut into chunks

CHICKEN PESTO PIZZA

Preheat oven to 450°F.

Spread pesto on pizza crust.

Top with chicken, artichoke hearts and grated cheese.

Sprinkle lightly with black pepper.

Bake 8–10 minutes until cheese is beginning to brown.

Prep time **5 minutes**   *Cook time* **8–10 minutes**

CEDAR PLANK SALMON (recipe on page 99)

"Old impotent Alden from Walden,
Ate salmon to heat him to scalding'!
Twas I was just the ticket, To stiffen his wicket,
The salmon of amorous Alden."

Anonymous

Salmon Seduction

Since this is a first date, don't overdo the romantic atmosphere. A fresh bouquet of flowers casually arranged, two candles in your candleholders and a dimmer switch are about all you need. Add the extra touch of picking up a greeting card while grocery shopping and place the card on your date's plate. The card should be a "getting to know you" card, one that can be found in the friends/lovers section. It should not be romantic (you're not there yet), funny or filled with sexual innuendoes. It should simply say "I like you and want to know you better."

GRILLED SALMON, CREAMY BAKED POTATOES WITH CHIVES SUMMER SALAD, CHAMPAGNE AND FRESH RASPBERRIES IN SPARKLING WINE

SHOPPING LIST

Produce
1^1/$_2$ tablespoons lemon juice

10 fresh raspberries for champagne

Grocery
2 teaspoons olive oil

1^1/$_2$ tablespoons capers

dash dry mustard

^{1}/$_4$ teaspoon salt

Seafood
2 salmon fillets

Liquor
1 tablespoon white wine for cooking

champagne or sparkling wine to drink

Miscellaneous
paper towels

GRILLED SALMON (opposite)

Pour a glass of champagne or sparkling wine.

Rinse salmon and pat dry with paper towels.

Combine remaining ingredients and mix well.

Pour over salmon and marinate for 30 minutes.

Grill or broil salmon for about 4 minutes on each side.

Baking the salmon in the lemon marinade is another option.

Prep time **35 minutes**   *Cook time* **10 minutes**

♡ One day before: Make dressing for salad. Make creamy chive mixture for potatoes. Cover each and refrigerate.

♡ One hour before: Bake potatoes. Turn off oven when they are done. Take chive mixture out of refrigerator.

♡ 45 minutes before: Prepare salmon for broiling, baking or grilling.

♡ 15 minutes before: Cook salmon. Make salads.

♡ 5 minutes before: Top potatoes with chive mixture. Drizzle dressing over salad.

♡ After dinner: Rinse raspberries, put a handful in 2 champagne flutes. Fill flutes with sparkling wine or champagne.

> "*Champagne ... takes its fitting rank and position (at a ball) amongst feathers, gavzes, lace, embroidery, ribbons, white satin shoes, and eau-de-Cologne, for champagne is simply one of the elegant extras of life.*"
>
> Charles Dickens

GRILLED SALMON (recipe on page 96)

SHOPPING LIST

Produce
2 large potatoes
1 tablespoon fresh chives

Grocery
1/3 teaspoon salt
dash of freshly ground pepper

Dairy
2 ounces goat cheese
(such as Montrachet)
1 tablespoon butter or margarine
1 tablespoon sour cream

CREAMY BAKED POTATOES WITH CHIVES

The night before, you can **combine** chives, salt, pepper, cheese, butter and sour cream. Refrigerate.

Bake potato at 350°F until done: (30–45 minutes).

Poke with knife to test for doneness.

Cut baked potato from end to end.

Spread potatoes open and top with creamy chive mixture.

Prep time **5 minutes**   *Cook time* **30–45 minutes**

"My idea of heaven is a great big baked potato and someone to share it with."

Oprah Winfrey

SHOPPING LIST

Produce
1/2 head butter lettuce
1 small ripe avocado, peeled and chopped
1 tomato, chopped
1 bunch fresh basil, chopped
1 teaspoon minced garlic

Grocery
2 tablespoons pine nuts, toasted
1 tablespoon white wine vinegar
2 teaspoons Dijon mustard
1 teaspoon honey
3 tablespoons olive oil
salt and pepper, to taste

SUMMER SALAD

Wash lettuce and drain in colander.

Tear lettuce into bite-sized pieces and place in large serving bowl.

Add avocado, tomato, basil and pine nuts.

Whisk vinegar, mustard, honey and garlic in a small bowl.

Add oil gradually, stirring constantly.

Season with salt and pepper.

Drizzle dressing over salad.

Prep time **10 minutes**

CEDAR PLANK SALMON, ARTICHOKE WITH BUTTER SAUCE, WILD LONG-GRAIN RICE, CHERRY ICE CREAM WITH FRESH CHERRIES AND MERLOT OR PINOT NOIR

This menu begins and ends with finger food! There is a correlation between the way a woman eats artichokes and her bedroom skills. Watching your partner dip an artichoke leaf in butter, then slowly pull the leaf through her teeth or suck a cherry off its stem suggests bedroom skills that men wait a lifetime to find.

Tell your date the history behind the cedar plank salmon. This dish began as an entrée for the Native Americans who lived in the Pacific Northwest. Since dinner conversation is sometimes difficult on a first dinner date at home, sharing this information can be fascinating.

SHOPPING LIST

Produce
3 lemons

Grocery
lemon pepper

Seafood
2 pieces 8 ounce salmon fillets with skin

Butcher Shop, Board Store or Michael's or call 1-800-881-1747
1 cedar board, 3 inches thick and 12 inches long

Liquor
merlot or pinot noir to drink

CEDAR PLANK SALMON (photograph on page 95)

The burning cedar creates the smoke that adds flavor to the salmon.

Soak cedar plank in water for 24 hours. **Place** salmon on cedar plank, skin-side down.

Squeeze juice of one lemon over the salmon.

Sprinkle lemon pepper over salmon.

Turn grill on high for a few minutes and then place board on the grill.

Close the hood and in about 5 minutes, squeeze juice of second lemon on salmon.

In about 15 minutes, depending on heat of grill and thickness of salmon, **remove** salmon from grill.

Place salmon on serving plate and garnish with slices of the third lemon.

*Prep time **24 hours**   Cook time **20 minutes***

♡ One day before: Soak cedar planks in water. Wash artichoke, cut off stem and trim leaves. Make dressing for salad. Cover and refrigerate.

♡ 60 minutes before: Cook artichoke. Wash cherries.

♡ 45 minutes before: Make salad.

♡ 30 minutes before: Cook salmon. Cook rice.

♡ After dinner: Serve ice cream and cherries.

SIRLOIN STEAK WITH PARSLEY BUTTER
(recipe on page 108)

Tom and Sue have been friends for years, supporting each other through
numerous personal and professional crises. Tom periodically suggests that
their relationship be less platonic. Sue's standard response is one that all guys
hate to hear: "Let's just be friends." One night when both are relationship- and
crisis-free, Tom fixes this steak dinner. At the end of dinner, Sue realizes that
she is bored beyond belief with all former lovers and that Tom is not only a
great cook, he makes her laugh and is exciting in bed. Fortunately, Tom's
sheets are clean.

"After all the trouble you go to, you get about as much actual 'food' out of eating an artichoke as you would from licking 30 or 40 postage stamps."

Miss Piggy

SHOPPING LIST

Produce
1 artichoke
2 tablespoons lemon juice

Dairy
4 ounces butter

Miscellaneous
kitchen scissors

ARTICHOKE WITH BUTTER SAUCE

Wash artichoke. Using kitchen scissors, cut off stem and trim leaves to about $^1/_4$ inch.

Snap off tough bottom row of leaves.

Place artichoke in a pot with about 3 inches of boiling water.

Add 1 tablespoon lemon juice.

Steam covered for about 45 minutes or until tender.

Drain and serve with butter sauce*.

Serve artichoke on a small plate.

Put butter sauce in a small bowl. Have an extra plate for the discarded artichoke leaves.

*Butter sauce: melt butter in small saucepan while artichoke is draining. Add 1 tablespoon lemon juice to butter.

Once all the leaves have been removed, the inedible prickly "choke" should be carefully cut or scraped away and discarded. What is left is the tender artichoke heart and meaty bottom. It's the best part of the artichoke.

Prep time **5 minutes**   *Cook time* **45 minutes**

> *"So we grew together, like to a double cherry, seeming parted,*
> *but yet an union in partition;*
> *Two lovely berries moulded on one stem."*
>
> William Shakespeare

SHOPPING LIST

Grocery
1 package wild long-grain rice

SHOPPING LIST

Produce
1 cup fresh cherries with stems

Frozen Desserts
cherry ice cream

WILD LONG-GRAIN RICE

Cook rice according to package directions.

FRESH CHERRIES AND ICE CREAM

Wash cherries, leaving stems on.

Scoop ice cream into two small bowls.

Put cherries in another serving bowl.

Pick up fresh cherries by the stem and eat with ice cream.

For breakfast, **serve** leftover cherries with toasted French bread and honey.

Prep time **5 minutes**

Jack finally got Anne to accept a dinner invitation to his home. While Anne admires Jack's intelligence, she never thought he was someone she would want to go to bed with. Anne, usually in complete control, almost got a case of the vapors over the salmon preparation. She discovered that intelligence and bedroom skills are not mutually exclusive. Jack also knows that Anne's artichoke and cherry eating skills were not false advertising.

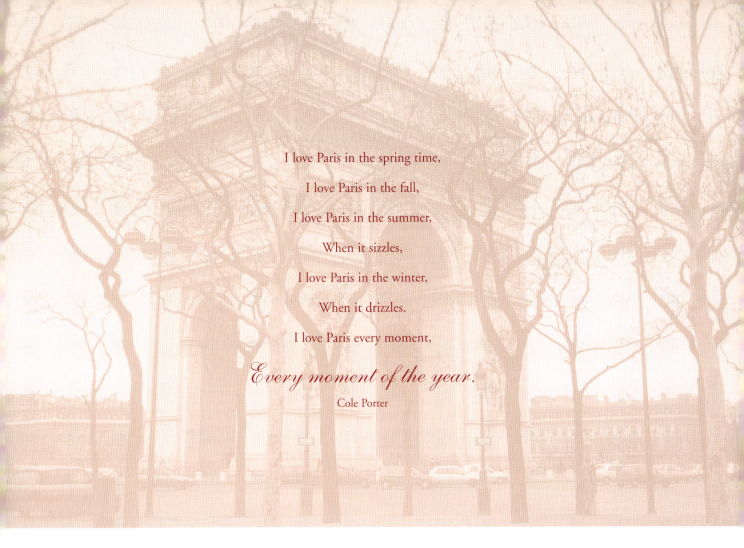

I love Paris in the spring time,

I love Paris in the fall,

I love Paris in the summer,

When it sizzles,

I love Paris in the winter,

When it drizzles.

I love Paris every moment,

Every moment of the year.

Cole Porter

A Taste of Paris Seduction

What could be more romantic than serving a "Taste of Paris" dinner? While we think of Paris in the spring time, this dinner can be served any season of the year. Frites (French fries) will be a big hit, as everyone loves them. As Joan Lunden says, "Show me a person who doesn't like French fries and we'll swap lies." You don't have to speak French to set a table that looks like an evening in Paris. All you need is a starched white tablecloth and napkins (both can be rented), a white candle and fresh flowers. Your date will believe you have the inimitable knack of turning a meal into a Parisian feast. Just add a bottle of wine. Well, maybe two bottles.

Ooh la la! This meal will put the taste of Paris on your table. The chocolate chip cookies will complete this bucolic evening.

SHOPPING LIST

Produce
1/3 cup green onions, minced

Grocery
1/2 teaspoon salt
4 teaspoons cracked pepper
1 tablespoon olive oil
1 tablespoon grainy mustard

Dairy
1/3 cup heavy cream

Meat
2 boneless sirloin steaks,
1 1/4 inch thick

Liquor
1/2 cup brandy for cooking
cabernet sauvignon to drink

NEW YORK STEAK AU POIVRE (opposite)

Heat skillet over high heat.

Pierce steak with fork and sprinkle with salt and pepper.

Heat oil in frying-pan; add steaks and cook for 6 minutes on each side.

Remove steaks, pour off fat and add green onions.

Cook and stir onions for 30 seconds.

Remove from skillet.

Add brandy and return to medium heat; cook 1 minute more.

Add cream and mustard and boil for 1–2 minutes.

Serve steaks with sauce poured over.

Prep time **5 minutes**   *Cook time* **20 minutes**

♡ One day before: Mince onions for steak and salad; put in a plastic bag. Refrigerate. Make vinaigrette. Poke holes in steak and sprinkle with salt and pepper.

♡ One hour before: Take steaks out of refrigerator. Wash and drain endive and parsley. Preheat oven to 400°F. Cut potatoes into wedges.

♡ 40 minutes before: Put potatoes in oven.

♡ 30 minutes before: Make salads and sauce for steaks.

♡ 20 minutes before: Start steaks. Place cookies on a serving plate.

"Beef is the soul of cooking"

Marie - Antoine Careme

SHOPPING LIST

Produce
*2 large baking potatoes,
cut lengthwise into wedges*

Grocery
*1 tablespoon vegetable oil
2 teaspoons seasoned salt
(Lowrey's seasoned salt)
¹/₄ teaspoon salt*

FRITES (above)

Preheat oven to 400°F.

Spread oil on cookie sheet.

Place potato wedges on sheet.

Sprinkle with seasoned salt; toss gently to coat.

Bake 40 minutes or until tender.

Sprinkle with salt and serve.

*Prep time **5 minutes**   Cook time **40+ minutes***

BISTRO SALAD (recipe on page 106)

(recipe on page 106)

SHOPPING LIST

Produce
2 cups endive
1 green onion, chopped

Grocery
red wine vinaigrette
1 cup croutons
¹/₈ teaspoon thyme, salt and pepper

Bakery
chocolate chip cookies

BISTRO SALAD (above)

Mix endive, onion and parsley in salad bowl.

Add herbs and seasoning to vinaigrette; shake.

Top with croutons.

Drizzle vinaigrette over salad and serve.

Prep time **10 minutes**

CHOCOLATE CHIP COOKIES

Serve with freshly brewed coffee.

MEN ONLY: KISS MY PALATE

"Roast Beef, Medium" is not only a food.
It is a philosophy safe and sane, and sure."

3.2 ENCORE EVENINGS

You have a great first date, with interesting and enlightening conversation. She indicates that she would like to see you again. This section will provide menus for encore evenings, as she *will be back*. If she wants to bring something, suggest that she bring flowers, a favorite dessert or a CD.

Steak/Salad/Martinis/Jazz

This is a great dinner for your jazz and martini aficionado as most women enjoy an evening that includes a little 'sax'. The martini, hands down, is the favored drink of fictional characters in movies and novels, and of politicians and movie stars. Soon she will be quoting Robert Benchley, "Why don't you slip out of those wet clothes and into a dry martini?"

Set the table with a white tablecloth, black napkins, martini glasses and shaker, silver serving dishes, black candles and white flowers. After dinner, entice your date to slow dance as slow dancing often leads to romance.

"I like a good martini, one or two at the most.
After one I'm under the table,
After two, I'm under the host."

Dorothy Parker

MEN ONLY: KISS MY PALATE ♥ 107

Sirloin Steak with Parsley Butter, Corn on the Cob, Caesar Salad and Martinis,

Shopping List

Produce
2 tablespoons fresh parsley, chopped

3 cloves garlic, chopped, or 3 teaspoons minced garlic

2 teaspoons lemon juice, freshly squeezed

Grocery
$^1/_8$ teaspoon salt and pepper

Dairy
4 ounces butter

Meat
2 sirloin steaks, about 6 ounces each

Sirloin Steak with Parsley Butter (photograph on page 100)

Pour a martini.

Preheat grill.

Combine butter, parsley, garlic, lemon juice, salt and pepper in a bowl.

Refrigerate butter mixture.

Season steaks with salt and pepper.

Grill steaks, turning once.

Cook for about 3 minutes each side for medium-rare.

Add 1 minute per side for medium.

Transfer steaks to serving platter and top each steak with a tablespoon of butter mixture. **Serve** immediately.

Prep time **5 minutes**   *Cook time* **4–6 minutes**

♡ One day before:. Make parsley butter for steaks.

♡ One hour before: Put salad plates in refrigerator.

♡ 30 minutes before: Start grill. Make Caesar salad

♡ 10 minutes before: Put steaks on the grill.

"People have tried and they have tried, but sex is not better than sweetcorn."

Garrison Keillor

CORN ON THE COB

An easy way to prepare corn on the cob is to buy it without husks.

Wash corn.

Bring a large kettle or pot of water (enough to cover the corn) to boiling.

Drop in corn.

Boil for 3–5 minutes.

Using tongs, **transfer** corn to a serving plate.

Put butter in a small bowl. Place salt, pepper and lemon pepper on the table. Corn with butter and lemon pepper is a great combination.

Prep time **1 minute**   *Cook time* **3–5 minutes**

CAESAR SALAD

Many grocery stores have packages of Caesar salad that includes all of the ingredients and dressing. Or, make this simple, yet impressive, recipe.

Place minced garlic, anchovies, olive oil, red wine vinegar and Worcestershire sauce in a wooden or glass mixing bowl.

Create a paste with two forks (break up the anchovies).

Add mustard, juice of $1/2$ lemon and mix.

Toss with lettuce, blending well.

Sprinkle with black pepper.

Put salad on chilled salad plates and top with croutons.

Prep time **10 minutes**

MARTINIS

A magazine once posed the question, "Is chocolate better than sex?"
A chocolate martini is a little of both. Add a Hershey's Chocolate Kiss and you have a relaxing dessert to end your evening.

SHOPPING LIST

Produce
1 lemon twist per drink

Liquor
6 parts vodka
1 part Chambord

Miscellaneous
cracked ice

SHOPPING LIST

Grocery
green exotic stuffed olives–pimento or garlic or almond or blue cheese

Liquor
6 parts gin
2 parts dry vermouth
1 part olive brine

Miscellaneous
cracked ice

CHAMBORD MARTINI

Combine vodka and Chambord in a cocktail shaker with cracked ice.

Shake well.

Strain into martini glasses.

Garnish with lemon twist.

DIRTY MARTINI

Place martini glasses in freezer for one hour.

Combine liquid ingredients in a cocktail shaker with cracked ice.

Shake well.

Strain into chilled martini glasses.

Add two or three olives.

> *"New York is the greatest city in the world for lunch.*
> *When that first martini hits the liver like a silver bullet,*
> *there is a huge sigh of contentment that can be heard in Dubuque."*
>
> William Emerson Jr.

SHOPPING LIST

Produce
1–2 melon balls per drink

Dairy
1 part fresh orange juice

Liquor
4 parts vodka
2 parts Midori liqueur

Miscellaneous
melon baller

SHOPPING LIST

Produce
1 lemon

Liquor
6 parts vodka
1 part Frangelico

SHOPPING LIST

Confectionery
1 Hershey's Chocolate Kiss

Liquor
6 parts vodka
1 part chocolate liqueur

Miscellaneous
ice

MELON BALL MARTINI

Shake juice and liquor over ice.

Pour into martini glasses.

Add a couple of melon balls per martini.

> *"A man must defend his wife,*
> *his home, his children and his Martini."*
>
> Jackie Gleason

NUTTY MARTINI

Combine vodka and Frangelico in a shaker with cracked ice.

Shake well.

Strain into chilled martini glasses and garnish with lemon.

At the end of dinner, she will be telling you, "You are the best thing about this evening, this month, this year."

CHOCOLATE KISS

Mix vodka and chocolate liqueur with ice.

Strain into martini glass.

Garnish with chocolate kiss.

Champagne Seduction, the Joy of Fizz

Champagne and shrimp, or chicken in champagne, along with a bottle of champagne to drink will be a great encore evening. Possibly it is your first month anniversary and you want to prepare a special dinner to celebrate. Champagne aficionados are winners, lovers and revellers who have been drenching themselves and imbibing champagne in the 20th and 21st centuries.

"You can have too much champagne to drink,
but you can never have enough."

Elmer Rice

CHAMPAGNE CHICKEN
(recipe on page 113)

SHOPPING LIST

Produce
*1 tablespoon fresh parsley,
chopped*

Grocery
salt and pepper
2^1/$_2$ tablespoons butter
1 tablespoon olive oil
*1^1/$_2$ tablespoons unbleached
all-purpose flour*
pinch rosemary and thyme
1 teaspoon dried tarragon
^{1}/$_2$ cup chicken broth

Dairy
^{1}/$_2$ cup heavy cream

Meat
4 boneless chicken breasts

Liquor
*1^3/$_4$ cups dry champagne for
recipe and rest of bottle for
drinking*

SHOPPING LIST

Produce
1 package greens

Grocery
vinaigrette of choice

CHAMPAGNE CHICKEN (opposite)

Pour a glass of champagne.

Sprinkle chicken breasts with salt and pepper.

Melt butter in frying-pan, add oil.

Brown breasts on both sides (about 10 minutes). **Remove** from pan and set aside.

Stir in the flour, rosemary, thyme and tarragon.

Cook for two minutes, stirring constantly.

Gradually **whisk** in 1 cup of champagne and the chicken broth. Return chicken to the pan.

Cover and simmer until chicken is tender (about 45 minutes).

Remove chicken to a warmed serving platter.

Stir in remaining champagne and the cream.

Cook sauce over high heat until reduced and slightly thickened.

Pour sauce over chicken, sprinkle with parsley and serve immediately in center of platter.

Prep time **5 minutes**   *Cook time* **1 hour**

♡ One hour fifteen minutes before: Make chicken in champagne.

♡ One hour before: Take cheesecake out of freezer, put slices on plates and top with washed strawberries.

♡ 30 minutes before: Cook fettuccini. Arrange greens on salad plates.

♡ 10 minutes before: Re-heat chicken. Drizzle vinaigrette over greens.

GREENS WITH VINAIGRETTE

Put greens on salad plates and drizzle with vinaigrette.

"Age is not important unless you are a cheese."

Helen Hayes (in the play *New Woman*)

SHOPPING LIST

Grocery
¹/₂ pound fettuccini

FETTUCCINI

Cook according to package directions.

Serve by pouring into a serving bowl or place around chicken breasts on platters.

SHOPPING LIST

Produce
¹/₂ cup fresh strawberries

Crust
6 ounces butter or margarine
1 cup Graham cracker crumbs
2 tablespoons brown sugar

Filling
3 packages (8 oz each) cream cheese softened
3 eggs lightly beaten
1 teaspoon lemon juice
1 cup sugar
2 teaspoons vanilla essence
2 cups sour cream

Miscellaneous
spring form pan

CHEESECAKE WITH STRAWBERRIES (opposite)

You can buy a cheesecake or make this recipe.

Melt butter in saucepan over medium heat.

Stir in crumbs and sugar.

Take a 10 inch springform tin and **pack** the mixture into sides and bottom to make a base.

Bake in oven at 325°F for 10 minutes.

To make filling **beat** cream cheese, eggs, sugar, lemon juice and vanilla together well. Then **mix** in sour cream.

Pour over crumb crust and bake in 325°F oven for 1 hour.

Let **stand** at least 2 hours.

Chill until ready to serve.

Use fresh strawberries to top the cheesecake.

CHEESECAKE WITH STRAWBERRIES
(recipe on page 114)

"Doubtless God could have made a berry,
but doubtless God never did."

William Butler (on the strawberry)

Bob, a retired engineer, is dating a woman 18 years younger than himself. When they first met, Rachel was reluctant to become involved with an older man. On a scale of 1–10, Rachel went off the scale. After several failed attempts, he won her over with this dinner. The menu was simple but ended with champagne, cheesecake and strawberries. They skipped cheesecake and took the champagne and strawberries to devour in Bob's bed. The next morning Bob served his new lover French toast and, yes leftover strawberries.

Shrimp in Champagne, Pasta, Greens with Walnuts and Goat Cheese, Chocolate Mousse and Champagne

Shopping List

Produce
1/2 cup sliced mushrooms

1 tablespoon green onions, minced

1 plum tomato, diced

Seafood
1 pound medium shrimp, shelled and deveined, tails removed

Grocery
1 tablespoon olive oil

pinch of salt

Dairy
1/4 cup heavy cream

Liquor
1/4 cup champagne for recipe, the rest for drinking

Miscellaneous
slotted spoon

Shrimp in Champagne (opposite)

Sauté mushrooms in a medium saucepan in hot olive oil over medium-high heat.

Cook just enough to soften mushrooms. Put them in a bowl and discard liquid.

Combine shrimp, champagne and salt in a saucepan.

On high heat, **cook** until liquid starts to boil; remove shrimp from liquid with slotted spoon when they are done (2–3 minutes).

Make sure you don't overcook.

Add shrimp to bowl with mushrooms.

Add green onions and tomatoes to the liquid in the saucepan.

Boil until liquid is reduced to 1/4 cup (about 8 minutes).

Add 1/4 cup of heavy cream and boil for 1–2 minutes until slightly thickened.

Add shrimp and mushrooms to sauce; heat through.

Add salt and pepper to taste.

Prep time **10 minutes**   *Cook time* **20 minutes**

♡ One day before: Make vinaigrette. Make chocolate mousse.

♡ One hour before: Make shrimp in champagne. Turn heat off and cover.

♡ 30 minutes before: Cook pasta. Combine greens and blue cheese. Take mousse out of refrigerator and pour into serving bowls and top with whipped cream.

♡ 10 minutes before: Re-heat shrimp. Drizzle vinaigrette over salads.

Shrimp and champagne are a dynamic duo that is too 'good' to miss!

SHRIMP IN CHAMPAGNE (recipe on page 116)

SHOPPING LIST

Produce
3 tablespoons fresh parsley, chopped

Grocery
¹/₂ pound angel hair pasta

Dairy
2 tablespoons heavy cream

PARSLEY PASTA

Cook pasta according to package directions.

Drain thoroughly and return to cooking pot.

Toss with cream and parsley.

To serve, **divide** pasta between two plates.

Spoon shrimp and sauce over pasta.

Prep time 5 minutes

"Lettuce is like conversation:
it must be fresh and crisp,
and so sparkling that you scarcely notice the bitter in it."

Charles Dudley Warner

SHOPPING LIST

Produce
1 package of salad greens

Grocery
2 tablespoons red wine vinegar
1 tablespoon Dijon mustard
1/4 cup vegetable oil
salt and freshly ground pepper
1 small can mandarin oranges, drained
juice of 1/2 orange

Dairy
goat cheese, crumbled

SHOPPING LIST

Grocery
1 package of instant chocolate mousse

Dairy
whipped cream
milk

GREENS WITH WALNUTS AND GOAT CHEESE

You can buy champagne vinaigrette and add a little orange juice or make the dressing below.

Combine vinegar, orange juice and mustard in small bowl and whisk well.

Slowly **drizzle** in the oil, whisking constantly until smooth.

Season with salt and pepper.

Put greens on a salad plate, top with mandarin orange slices, goat cheese and walnuts.

Pour vinaigrette over salad so lightly covered.

Prep time **15 minutes**

CHOCOLATE MOUSSE (opposite)

You can make this chocolate mousse. A simpler dessert, serve a sweeter champagne, like Asti spumanti, and chocolates or just serve Chambord.

Make mousse according to package directions.

Top with whipped cream.

John and Nita play nine holes of golf. Their score cards are filled with beer stains and XOXOXOXOX because their golf scores really suck. John invites Nita to his place, cooks this dinner and then really scores. Over breakfast, Nita tells John that golf and sex are two things *you don't have to be good at to enjoy.*

"Life is a combination of, magic and pasta"

Federico Fellini

CHOCOLATE MOUSSE (recipe on page 118)

Vealing Darling?

Your date has been working around the clock to meet ridiculous deadlines. Her final project has to be completed no later than noon on Friday. She lets you know that she will be in bed by 7:00 pm. on Friday night. When she stumbles out of bed on Saturday, you have breakfast ready. A masseuse comes to your house and gives both of you massages. Your date crawls back into bed with a book while listening to new-age music, Enya and Krishna Das. Fresh flowers and aroma therapy candles surround the bed. You fix this light evening meal that goes with a spa day.

Shrimp Boiled in Shells, Veal with Lemon Capers, Vegetable Linguine, Strawberries with Brown Sugar and Sour Cream, and Pinot Noir or Burgundy

Shopping List

Grocery
1 package shrimp boil
1 jar cocktail sauce

Seafood
1/2 pound large shrimp

Liquor
pinot noir or Burgundy
to drink

Eating shrimp is very casual eating. Have plenty of napkins for this one. But after having your body lathered with massage oil, who cares if your fingers get a bit messy.

Shrimp Boiled in Shells

Fill a medium saucepan half full of water. **Bring** water to boil.

Add shrimp boil when water is boiling vigorously.

Add shrimp and boil for 3–5 minutes. Shrimp will be pink when done.

Drain in colander then immediately run cold tap water over shrimp.

Pour cocktail sauce into a small bowl.

Serve shrimp with cocktail sauce.

Prep time **1 minute**   *Cook time* **3–5 minutes**

♡ One day before: Slice vegetables and make parsley puree for vegetable linguine. Cover and refrigerate. Mix brown sugar and sour cream, cover and refrigerate.

♡ 45 minutes before: Wash strawberries. Take brown sugar and sour cream out of refrigerator.

♡ 30 minutes before: Make vegetable linguine, turn off heat. Keep covered.

♡ 20 minutes before: Make veal with lemon capers. Turn off heat; keep covered.

♡ 10 minutes before: Cook shrimp. Pour cocktail sauce into bowl.

SHOPPING LIST

Produce
2 tablespoons fresh lemon juice
lemon slices for garnish
1 tablespoon fresh chopped
parsley

Grocery
1 tablespoon all-purpose flour
1/4 teaspoon salt
1/4 teaspoon freshly ground
black pepper
2 teaspoons olive oil
1/2 cup salt-reduced chicken
broth
1 tablespoon capers, drained
and rinsed

Meat
1/2 pound veal scallops

VEAL WITH LEMON CAPERS (above)

Combine flour, salt and pepper on a plate.

Coat one side of each veal scallop with flour mixture; set aside.

Heat oil in medium non-stick frying-pan; add veal, flour-side down.

Cook over medium-high heat for 1 minute on each side until lightly browned and cooked through.

Remove veal from frying-pan and set aside.

Combine lemon juice, parsley, broth and capers in same frying-pan.

Bring to boil over high heat. Cook for 2 minutes until liquid is reduced in volume to about 1/3 cup.

Return veal and any accumulated juices to frying-pan; cook, turning as needed, just until heated through.

Serve on platter, pour liquid from pan over veal.

*Prep time **10 minutes**   Cook time **15 minutes***

VEGETABLE LINGUINE (recipe on page 122)

SHOPPING LIST

Produce
4 medium carrots
1 medium zucchini
1 medium yellow squash
¹/2 cup fresh parsley
2 tablespoons fresh basil
1 teaspoon minced garlic or
1 clove garlic

Grocery
1 cup chicken broth
6 ounces linguine
1 tablespoon olive oil
¹/8 teaspoon ground pepper

Dairy
³/4 cup grated Parmesan cheese

SHOPPING LIST

Produce
12 large strawberries with stems

Grocery
¹/4 cup brown sugar

Dairy
¹/4 cup sour cream

VEGETABLE LINGUINE (above)

Slice carrots, zucchini and yellow squash into long strands. **Set** aside.

Purée parsley, broth, basil, oil and garlic in blender or food processor.

Put a large pot of water on the stove over medium heat.

Add linguine to boiling water and cook for 5 minutes.

Add carrots and cook for 5 minutes.

Add zucchini and yellow squash strands to linguine–carrot mixture; drain immediately.

Add parsley mixture; toss to combine.

Serve with Parmesan and pepper.

*Prep time **15–20 minutes**   Cook time **12–15 minutes***

STRAWBERRIES WITH BROWN SUGAR AND SOUR CREAM

Mix sour cream with sugar.

Wash strawberries and place them in a serving bowl.

Serve brown sugar and crfeam mixture seperately in a small bowl.

Dip strawberries in sour cream and brown sugar, eating one at a time.

*Prep time **2 minutes***

122   MEN ONLY: KISS MY PALATE

What's Love Got to Do with It?

Cocoa has been around for thousands of years and so has the legend that it is an aphrodisiac. Montezuma, ruler of those passionate Aztecs, supposedly downed fifty cups of hot cocoa before having sex with several of six hundred concubines. Chocolate contains PEA (phenylethyl-amine), the same endorphin released in the bloodstream when you fall in love. It also contains the stimulant caffeine and theobromine, which should keep your lady from falling asleep after dinner. Women crave sweet foods and fat, especially when suffering from PMS when serotonin levels dip. If your date is blue, lethargic or testy, chocolate kisses are the perfect antidote. If she still has PMS after eating the kisses, send her home. Experience this provacative combination of bursting Beaujolais and contemporary grilled filets for a "Two to Tango" evening.

Setting the scene: When she arrives, have chocolate almond kisses on the floor symbolizing that you "kiss the ground" she walks on. Cover the dining room table with heart-shaped chocolates. This is especially striking on a dark wood table. Put heart-shaped chocolate wrapped in colored foil on the table or in bowls. Write her a check for a million kisses and let her take it to the bank. Sparkling wines with a touch of sweetness, Asti Spumante or Mum's extra dry champagne, are the recommended bubbly to accompany the chocolate. Wear your favorite glow-in-the-dark Valentine underwear when serving dessert. Possibly a pair that says "Loves Me? Loves Me Hot!" Take a chocolate aromatic bath together. Spoon 3 tablespoons cocoa powder and 1 tablespoon of powdered milk under warm running water and jump in. A sweet ending that is sticky and sexy. Splashing will stir up the hot chocolate bath.

FILET MIGNON (recipe on page 123)

FILET MIGNON, POTATO GRATIN, BEAUJOLAIS OR CABERNET SAUVIGNON OR MERLOT, CREAMY CHOCOLATE-RASPBERRY FONDUE, AND ASTI SPUMANTE

SHOPPING LIST

Meat
2 filet mignons, 8 ounces each and 2 inches thick

Grocery
salt and pepper

Liquor
Beaujolais or cabernet sauvignon or merlot to drink

SHOPPING LIST

Produce
2 baking potatoes, peeled and sliced

Grocery
1/2 teaspoon salt
pinch of freshly ground pepper

Dairy
1/2 cup grated Gruyère cheese
1/4 cup heavy cream
1 1/4 tablespoons butter

Liquor
1 can beer

THE MAIN EVENT: FILET MIGNON (photograph on page 123)

Sprinkle salt and pepper on filets.

Grill steaks for 4 minutes. **Turn** and **grill** for another 3 minutes for rare meat.

For medium, **cook** an additional minute on each side.

*Prep time **5 minutes**   Cook time **7–10 minutes***

♡ Day before: Make chocolate sauce. Refrigerate covered.

♡ One hour before: Prepare potatoes. Turn oven to 375°F.

♡ 50 minutes before: Prepare and bake potatoes.

♡ 30 minutes before: Wash and prepare fruit and cake for dessert. Cover with plastic wrap. Start grill.

♡ 10 minutes before: Grill steaks.

SUPPORTING PLAYERS: POTATO GRATIN (photograph on page 123)

Preheat oven to 375°F.

Grease glass baking dish with butter.

Slice potatoes about 1/4 inch thick and put in baking dish.

Sprinkle with salt and pepper.

Pour beer over, just covering potatoes.

Bake for about 30 minutes, until potatoes are tender.

Add grated cheese and cream, and top with butter.

Return to oven, baking until top is brown.

Cool for 10–15 minutes before serving.

*Prep time **10 minutes**   Cook time **40 minutes***

CREAMY CHOCOLATE-RASPBERRY FONDUE
(recipe on page 125)

Produce for dipping
fresh strawberries, pineapple cubes, kiwi and fresh or dried apricots

Grocery
6 ounces dark chocolate chips
2–3 tablespoons raspberry liqueur or raspberry syrup
pinch of salt

Frozen Desserts
1 pound cake

Dairy
6 ounces cream cheese, softened
1/2 cup milk

Miscellaneous
fondue pot
2 dippers

GRAND FINALE: CREAMY CHOCOLATE-RASPBERRY FONDUE (above)

You probably missed the swinging sixties when fondue pots were popular. So you will probably have to buy a fondue pot and dippers for this evening as fondue pots are again hip. It is considered the ultimate fast food. When your date drops the dipper she has to kiss the host. You can serve the Asti spumante with dessert or save it for your soak in the chocolate aromatic bath together.

Combine chocolate chips, cream cheese, milk and raspberry liqueur or syrup.

Stir constantly until mixture is melted and smooth.

Transfer to fondue pot or bowl.

Serve with fruit and bite-sized pieces of cake for dipping. Long forks can be used for dipping.

Good dippers include strawberries, fresh pineapple cubes, kiwi, dried or fresh apricots, and pound cake. Just have 2–3 of these for dipping. Sauce can be made 2–3 days ahead, storing covered in refrigerator. Gently reheat to serve.

Prep time **15 minutes**   *Cook time* **5 minutes**

"Too much of a good thing is wonderful"

Mae West

BEEF BURGUNDY, NOODLES, GREENS, CHOCOLATE ICE CREAM, AND PINOT NOIR OR MERLOT

SHOPPING LIST

Produce
2 medium onions, quartered
$^1/_2$ pound fresh mushrooms

Grocery
1 tablespoon oil
1 teaspoon butter or margarine
2 teaspoons flour
pinch of salt and pepper
$^1/_3$ cup beef broth

Meat
1-1$^1/_2$ pounds lean chuck steak, cubed (ask the butcher to do this) Buy prime beef.

Wine
$^1/_3$ cup red wine to cook
pinot noir or merlot to drink

BEEF BURGUNDY (opposite)

A beef dish that will put the "aah" into your relationship.

Pour a glass of wine.

Sauté onions in butter or margarine until light brown. Remove.

Add oil and meat. Brown well.

Add flour, salt and pepper.

Stir well until smooth and brown.

Add beef broth and wine.

Simmer for 1$^1/_2$ hours.

Add mushrooms and cook for 45 minutes.

Beef burgundy will taste better if cooked one day before. If cooking one day before, cook for $^1/_2$ hour less.

Prep time **15 minutes**   *Cook time* **45 minutes**

♡ One day before: Make beef burgundy. Refrigerate in covered container. Make walnut oil for salad.

♡ One hour before: Make salads.

♡ 30 minutes before: Re-heat beef burgundy. Cook noodles, cover and turn off heat.

♡ Take ice cream out of freezer 15 minutes before serving.

SHOPPING LIST

Grocery
1 packet of noodles

Dairy
1 tablespoon butter

NOODLES

Cook according to package directions.

Stir butter through cooked noodles.

SHOPPING LIST

Produce
1 teaspoon chopped fresh rosemary or ¹/₂ teaspoon dried rosemary, crushed
2 tablespoons lemon juice
8 ounces mixed spring salad greens

Grocery
3 tablespoons extra virgin olive oil
¹/₄ teaspoon salt and ground black pepper
¹/₂ cup walnuts

Dairy
¹/₄ cup shaved Parmesan cheese (optional)

SHOPPING LIST

Produce
1 pint rich chocolate ice cream

GREENS WITH WARM WALNUT DRESSING

Combine rosemary and olive oil in a small saucepan.

Place on medium-low heat and let infuse for 5 minutes.

Remove from heat.

Whisk in lemon juice, salt and pepper.

Stir in walnuts. Chill.

Pour over salad greens, toss gently and transfer to plates.

If using Parmesan, **sprinkle** over each salad. **Serve.**

Prep time **15 minutes**

CHOCOLATE ICE CREAM

For real decadence, eat the ice cream right out of the container in the living room or bedroom. Have 2 spoons. This touch will "charge" your date's circuits.

Nobody knows the truffles I've seen

You ask a co-worker you find attractive to a Super Bowl party. Your date loves football and seems to know something about each team. It is the second half before you figure out which team is wearing the dark jerseys, as you are football challenged. To get a second date with her, you bet a steak dinner on the game, letting her choose the winner. Set the stakes high, this dinner, and hope you lose the bet and win at romance.

SHOPPING LIST

Produce
1 cup snow peas

Grocery
salt and pepper

Meat
2 bacon-wrapped filets

Frozen Vegetables
2 twice baked potatoes

Dairy
1 teaspoon butter

liquor
shiraz to drink

Confectionery
chocolate truffles

BACON-WRAPPED FILETS, SNOW PEAS, POTATOES AND TRUFFLES (opposite)

Sprinkle filets with salt and pepper.

Grill filets for 4 minutes one side, 3 minutes on the other for rare. For medium, **cook** an additional minute on each side. Alternatively, you can **cook** in olive oil and butter in a heavy frying-pan.

Microwave snow peas for 2–3 minutes. **Remove** and put 1 teaspoon butter on top and **cover**. **Sprinkle** with salt and pepper.

Microwave or bake twice baked potatoes according to directions.

Put filets and twice baked potatoes on a serving plate.

Pour peas into a serving bowl. **Put** truffles on a dessert plate and **serve** after dinner.

Prep time **5 minutes**   *Cook time* **10 minutes**

♡ 30 minutes before: Put truffles on dessert plate and set aside.

♡ 15 minutes before: Preheat grill. Cook filets.

♡ 10 minutes before: Microwave potatoes and cover until ready to serve.

♡ 5 minutes before: Microwave peas, top with butter and cover.

"*The truffle is not a positive aphrodisiac, but it can upon occasion make women tenderer and men more apt to love.*"

Jean-Anthelme Brillat-Savarin

BACON-WRAPPED FILETS, SNOW PEAS, POTATOES AND TRUFFLES
(recipe on page 128)

STEAMED SHRIMP, OVEN-BAKED POTATO WEDGES, CHOCOLATE BROWNIES AND CHARDONNAY
(THIS IS A "NO TIME TO COOK" MEAL.)

SHOPPING LIST

Fish
2 pounds fresh green shrimp

Frozen Vegetables
1 package of oven baked potato wedges

Dairy
1 tablespoon butter

Fresh Desserts
2 brownies

Liquor
chardonnay to drink

Miscellaneous
bamboo steamer

STEAMED SHRIMP (opposite)

Cook shrimp in a bamboo steamer over a saucepan of boiling water.

Heat potato wedges in oven according to package directions.

Serve shrimp and wedges in serving dishes.

Put brownies on dessert plates.

Prep time **5 minutes**   *Cook time* **10–15 minutes**

♡ One hour before: Take shrimp and potatoes out of the refrigerator.

♡ 30 minutes before: Place chocolate cookies on plates.

♡ 15 minutes before: Steam shrimps and bake potato wedges.

Meg and Peter meet when both miss their connecting flights and they spend three hours in the St. Louis airport bar. Peter is immediately attracted to Meg as she is a very beautiful lady. Everyone in the bar is watching the first round of the NCAA Basketball Tournament. Between the hoops and the whoops, Peter and Meg start talking. Peter is in television and Meg is a recruiter. Peter quickly learns that Meg isn't just another pretty interface. She is conversant on all of the important acronyms – NBA, NHL, PGA, WWF and NFL. They soon discover both live in the Quad Cities and have lots of common interests besides sports. Before they land in Moline, they exchange telephone numbers and agree to get together soon. Once back home, Peter assumes Meg is experiencing a touch of "March Madness" when she said she wants to see him again. She probably won't even return his telephone calls. Peter decides to take a chance and invite her to the St Patrick's Day Parade. They go to the parade, drink green beer, eat corned beef and cabbage and watch the second round of the NCAA tournament in their favorite Irish pub.

Both have such a great time that Meg accepts an invitation to Peter's place for this dinner and to watch a movie. By the end of March, they are spending every weekend and a couple of nights during the week together. After three months, Peter suggests they live together.

STEAMED SHRIMP (recipe on page 130)

He thinks Meg's reluctance is fear of commitment. Instead, Meg just can't find a way to tell Peter that she can't cook. When she confesses her deficiency, Peter assures her they can work it out. They are still together after two years and marriage is imminent.

STEAK AND RED PEPPERS (recipe on page 133)

American Beauty Evening

Your date has been working late nights, early mornings, having meetings about meetings – life is beyond frenzied. Re-energize her with an American Beauty Evening. This evening will smooth out life's edges. Red roses on the dining room table with a white tablecloth or place mats and white dishes or off-white dishes and an off-white tablecloth. This will make your red roses the focal point.

After dinner fill the bathtub with water and add bath oil. Sprinkle the red rose petals on the water. You can clean the kitchen while she soaks. Put her towel and terry robe in the dryer so they will be warm when she finishes her soak. Save some of the rose petals to place on her chest for love-making. The soft, sensual scent is a wonderful experience for both partners.

STEAK AND RED PEPPERS, ASPARAGUS EROTICA, ROQUEFORT POTATOES, FRENCH BORDEAUX OR AUSTRALIAN SHIRAZ, STRAWBERRIES, AND CHAMPAGNE

SHOPPING LIST

Produce
1 red and 1 yellow pepper, seeded and cut into various sized heart shapes
4 teaspoons minced garlic
1 diced shallot

Grocery
3 tablespoons olive oil
2 teaspoons balsamic vinegar
1/2 teaspoon sugar
salt and freshly ground pepper
3 tablespoons sun-dried tomatoes, packed in oil

Meat
1 pound sirloin steak

Confectionary
bag of heart-shaped candy

Liquor
French Bordeaux or Australian shiraz to drink

The combination of wonderful food, heart-shaped candy, heart-shaped peppers and several bottles of wine can lead to a marriage proposal when you only intended to ask her to sleep over. If you don't want this to happen, skip the heart-shaped peppers and go easy on the wine.

STEAK AND RED PEPPERS (opposite)

Heat oil in large skillet over medium heat.

Add heart shaped peppers and shallot and sauté for 10 minutes.

Add garlic and sauté for 5 minutes.

Stir in vinegar and sugar. **Add** salt and pepper to taste.

Cook uncovered over medium heat, stirring occasionally, for 15 minutes.

Stir in drained tomatoes.

Simmer for 2 minutes.

Sprinkle salt and pepper over steaks.

Grill steaks or cook them in heavy frying-pan with olive oil and butter.

The red pepper sauce can be made ahead and re-heated while you are grilling the steaks. If you do not have a stove-top grill, you can cook the steaks in butter or olive oil in a heavy frying-pan on the stove.

Prep time **15 minutes** *Cook time* **50 minutes**

♡ One day before: Make potatoes, cover and refrigerate. Scald, peel and core tomatoes. Cover and refrigerate overnight.

♡ One hour before: Take potatoes, steak and strawberries out of the refrigerator. Make red pepper sauce. Turn off. Put washed strawberries in a bowl. Pour candy into a bowl. Cook asparagus. Put asparagus erotica together in baking dish. Preheat oven.

♡ 30 minutes before: Put asparagus in oven. Heat grill.

♡ 15 Minutes Before: Heat potatoes on low heat. Cook steaks.

"*In the nineteenth century it was traditional to serve three courses of asparagus—thought to be a powerful aphrodisiac—to the French groom the night before the wedding. The modern Frenchman has discarded the noble asparagus for the more romantic passion prompter—champagne.*"

Sharon Tyler Herbst

SHOPPING LIST

Produce
12 small asparagus stalks
2 medium tomatoes

Grocery
1/8 teaspoon salt and pepper
2 tablespoons bread crumbs

Dairy
2 tablespoons melted butter
2 tablespoons Romano cheese

ASPARAGUS EROTICA (opposite)

Asparagus is such an exquisite vegetable and this particular recipe is very provocative. It is also a good source of potassium, essential for optimal energy. This recipe will take a little more time, but the presentation will be well worth it. If you prefer a simpler alternative, microwave fresh asparagus wrapped in plastic wrap for $1^1/2$ minutes. Drizzle with butter and sprinkle with salt and pepper or lemon pepper.

Pour a glass of wine.

Preheat oven to 350°F.

Cut 1 inch from the bottom of the asparagus.

Blanch asparagus in salted water until nearly tender (30 seconds to a minute).

Put in colander and cool with cold tap water. Drain.

Core tomatoes. **Place** tomatoes in baking dish.

Dip cooked asparagus in melted butter.

Stand 5–6 stalks of asparagus in each tomato.

Pour remaining butter over tomato.

Sprinkle with breadcrumbs and cheese.

Bake for 25 minutes.

Prep time **15 minutes**   *Cook time* **35 minutes**

"*No Agnes,*
        Bordeaux is not a house of ill repute"

George Bain

"Just give me a potato, any kind of potato, and I'm happy."

Dolly Parton

Produce

2 pounds small red potatoes

1/4 cup fresh parsley, chopped (optional)

Grocery

1/2 teaspoon salt and freshly ground pepper

Dairy

1/3 cup crumbled Roquefort or blue cheese

3 tablespoons freshly grated Parmesan cheese (optional)

1/4 cup sour cream

1 tablespoon butter (optional)

ROQUEFORT POTATOES (photograph on page 135)

While this recipe is orgasmic, a simpler preparation is cutting small red potatoes in half and cooking in boiling water until done. Sprinkle with salt and pepper. When you serve, toss a handful of crumbled Roquefort or blue cheese over the potatoes.

Cut potatoes in quarters and put them in a medium saucepan.

Cover with water and cook until tender (about 15 minutes).

Coarsely **mash** potatoes with an electric mixer or a potato masher.

Add cheese and sour cream.

Mash again until smoother, but still coarse.

Add butter and season with salt and pepper.

The potatoes will be fairly smooth with flecks of red skin. They can be made the day before and re-heated, covered, on low heat or in the microwave. Sprinkle with parsley and serve.

Prep time **10 minutes**   *Cook time* **15 minutes**

"Potatoes in the dining room,
Frolic in the bedroom."

Author Unknown

SHOPPING LIST

Produce
1 pound of fresh strawberries

Liquor
1 bottle of champagne or dessert wine

STRAWBERRIES AND CHAMPAGNE

Strawberries are an aphrodisiac; they are the ultimate "let me feed you" food. Tell your date that her lips remind you of ripe strawberries.

Wash strawberries, leave the stems on.

Put strawberries in a bowl and pop the champagne cork.

Prep time **5 minutes**

"Champagne is the wine lovers luxury."

Jancis Robinson

John was shopping in his favorite grocery store where he is now on a first-name basis with the florist, the meat cutter and the wine buyer. When John arrived with his shopping list for this dinner, the florist asked, "Who is it this time?" John responded that he had found someone with the trinity – great mind, great body and great face. The florist's immediate response was that she had heard this before and the description sounded like his last four dream dates. John's new love writes for an advertising agency and she could be in the ads rather than writing them. This dinner was just the ticket to win her heart.

Chapter 4 : Morning-After Breakfasts

4

"If this is coffee, please bring me some tea;
if this is tea, please bring me some coffee."

Abraham Lincoln

You and your date enjoy an evening of romance and she stays over. You like each other and your relationship is developing into something special, possibly picking up momentum. She wants to have breakfast at your place instead of at Tiffany's. The next step is preparing breakfast. Be sure to have coffee and a variety of teas to choose from. Breakfast can be as simple as coffee or tea and toast or cereal. This would be a good time to pull out your grandmother's Wedgwood china cups, saucers and bowls. If your grandmother didn't leave her china to you, have some entertaining-only dinnerware for two. Serving her breakfast in bed will provide assurance that you respect her in the morning.

If she is a Java junkie, she is probably a Type A personality. Coffee is a jolt, a jump-start, a recharge, a drink for people with drive. Coffee drinkers do not have time to stand around holding a little bag on a string, waiting for the water to turn the color of pantyhose. Coffee drinkers are "on the move, they need fuel, there's a sense of urgency to them" (Roger Scheumann, owner of Quartermaine Coffee Roasters).

Tea drinkers are Type B. The image of tea drinkers is serene and relaxed and inhabiting some higher cerebral plain than coffee drinkers. Tea drinkers in this country are urban and affected and a lot more defensive about their choice of beverage.

The Creoles describe coffee as black as the devil, strong as death, sweet as love and hot as hell. If your date is like Steve Martin in *L. A. Story* and asks you for a "half double decaffeinated half cup with a twist of lemon", consider going out for coffee or sending her home.

Coffee tips:

♡ buy quality dark-roasted beans

♡ make coffee strong and flavorful

♡ serve immediately as coffee sitting on a burner for hours tastes like kerosene

SHOPPING LIST

Grocery
coffee beans, a dark roast
cherry jelly
sugar and sweetener

Bakery
1 loaf whole grain bread

Dairy
low-fat margarine
skim milk, half and half

TOAST, CHERRY JELLY, SKINNY LATTE

Make coffee, **toast** and **serve** immediately with margarine and jelly.

Prep time **10 minutes**

*"The morning cup of coffee
has an exhilaration about it which
the cheering influence of
the afternoon or evening cup of tea
cannot be expected to reproduce."*

Oliver Wendell Homes, Sr.

TOAST

All around the country and coast to coast,

People always say what do you like most?

I don't want to brag and I don't want to boast.

I always tell them I like toast.

Yeah toast! Yeah toast!

I get up in the morning about 6 am,

Have a little jelly, have a little jam.

Take a piece of bread, put it in the slot.

Push down the lever and the wire gets hot.

I get toast.

Yeah toast! Yeah toast!

Now there's no secret to toasting to perfection,

There's a dial on the side to make your selection.

Push to the dark or to the light,

And then if it pops too soon,

Push down again and make toast.

Yeah toast! Yeah toast!

When the first cavemen came in from the dregs,

Didn't know what would go with the bacon and the eggs.

Must have been a genius, got it in the head.

Plug in the toaster, bought a bag of bread.

Yeah toast! Yeah toast

Haywood Banks

The author is obviously a toast lover and looks forward to any breakfast that includes quality multi-grain breads.

SHOPPING LIST

Grocery
1 small can diced green chilies

Dairy
margarine or butter
4 eggs
1 1/2 cups milk
8 ounces grated Monterey Jack
8 ounces grated Cheddar

SHOPPING LIST

Grocery
1 package cornbread mix
(check package for additional
ingredients like milk and eggs)
honey

Dairy
butter or low-fat margarine

CHILI RELLENOS (below)

Preheat oven to 350°F.

Grease baking dish with margarine.

Whisk eggs, add milk, cheese and chilies.

Pour into baking dish and bake for 30 minutes.

Prep time **15 minutes**   *Cook time* **30 minutes**

♡ One day before: Combine ingredients for chilli rellenos. Make cornbread.

CORNBREAD

You can bake cornbread or buy frozen cornbread and thaw to room temperature.

Bake according to directions.

Serve hot cornbread with butter and honey.

CHILI RELLENOS (recipe on page 141)

Grocery
1 box of shredded wheat biscuits
1 cup Kellog's Product 19
1 cup all bran
1 cup rolled oats
$1/2$ cup wheat germ
$1/3$ cup raisins
$1/3$ cup sliced or chopped almonds
$1/2$ cup sunflower seeds
$1/3$ cup sesame seeds

Tea
green or chai tea

Dairy
skim milk or light soy milk

SHOPPING LIST

Produce
cantaloupe (cubed)
blueberries

Bakery
2–4 fresh muffins

Frozen Food
1 frozen quiche or quiche filling
and a pie shell

Dairy
margarine or butter

SHOPPING LIST

Produce
1 ripe banana
$3/4$ pound strawberries

Dairy
$1/2$ cup low-fat vanilla yogurt
1 quart orange juice to drink

SUPER CEREAL

A simpler breakfast is to select a couple of your favorite breakfast cereals and serve with banana and skim milk.

Toss cereals, dried fruit and nuts by hand in a large container.

Store in an airtight container.

Serve with skim milk or light soy milk.

Top with sliced banana.

Prep time **5 minutes**

You can substitute your favorite cereals for the ones listed above; just don't include sugar-coated cereals.

"All happiness depends on a leisurely breakfast."

John Gunther

CHEESE QUICHE, FRESH FRUIT AND MUFFINS

The frozen section of your supermarket has ready-to-bake quiches. It also has frozen quiche filling. Just thaw and bake.

You can create your own signature quiche simply by adding your favorite meat or vegetables or both. You could add cooked sausage, fresh or canned mushrooms, salmon, cooked shrimp, diced chicken, cubed ham, crumbled bacon, chopped green pepper, cooked hash browns, chopped broccoli, etc.

Cube cantaloupe and combine with blueberries in a serving bowl.

Warm muffins in the oven at 300°F.

Put a napkin in a basket and place warm muffins in the basket just before serving.

Serve with margarine or butter.

Prep time **15 minutes**   *Cooking time* **See package directions**

STRAWBERRY SMOOTHIE AND ORANGE JUICE

Blend banana, strawberries, yogurt and pour into glasses.

Serve smoothie and orange juice

Prep time **5 minutes**

BAGELS WITH SMOKED SALMON AND CREAM CHEESE,
BLOODY MARY (recipe on page 143)

(recipe on page 143)

(recipe on page 143)

SHOPPING LIST

Meat
smoked salmon

Dairy
cream cheese

Bakery
bagels

liquor
vodka
Bloody Mary mix

Miscellaneous
favorite morning newspaper

BAGELS WITH SMOKED SALMON AND CREAM CHEESE, BLOODY MARY, AND A FAVORITE MORNING NEWSPAPER (above)

Put smoked salmon on a small plate with a butter knife.

Use a table knife to soften cream cheese and then **transfer** to small bowl for serving.

Make Bloody Marys.

Put a napkin in a basket.

Place sliced bagels in the basket.

Prep time **10 minutes**

Chapter 5: Other Romantic Interlude

5

5.1 POSH PICNICS

Since the nineteenth century, picnics have offered an acceptable opportunity for promiscuous intermingling of the sexes. Picnics go 21st century with a thoroughly modern backpack that is full of things you need to eat, drink and be merry. Picnics are no longer just a summer activity as the serene setting can be your bedroom in December.

Most people envision a beach when planning a picnic. City parks and rooftops can be a beach alternative. Let your imagination run wild and dream up new reasons and places to have a picnic: dragon boat races; water skiing shows; by an ocean, lake, river or pond; concert in the park; tennis match; fireworks on 4th July; biking; cross-country skiing; or walking. This cookbook includes recipes for summer and fall biking, after cross-country skiing and a picnic on your bed in December.

Picnic essentials:

♡ Plates, glassware, utensils, spoons, forks, serving spoons.

♡ A blanket or quilt to sit and eat on.

♡ Napkins, preferably cloth. Bring extras in case of spills.

♡ Garbage bag for waste.

♡ Picnic basket or backpack.

♡ Insulated containers (for hot or cold drinks).

♡ Corkscrew if wine is to be served.

♡ No cell phones are allowed.

♡ Most important: great food and wonderful company.

Baggage stores sell a backpack picnic set with knives, forks, plastic plates and wine glasses, plus 2 insulated bottle coolers, 1 removable insulated hot pouch, 2 serving containers, tablecloth with napkins, can opener and bottle opener.

Avocado Sandwiches, Cheese and Crackers, Sliced Peaches and Blueberries or Watermellon and Blueberries, and Bottled Water, Iced Tea or Pinot Noir

SHOPPING LIST

Produce
1 ripe avocado
$^1/_2$ teaspoon lemon juice

Grocery
salt and pepper

Meat
$^1/_2$ pound pre-cooked bacon

Bakery
4 slices whole wheat or multi-grain bread

Miscellaneous
paper towels
plastic bags

AVOCADO SANDWICHES

The lusty Aztecs dubbed the avocado as an overpowering aphrodisiac. When the avocado was harvested, Aztec maidens were forbidden from going outside. And you thought it was the margarita that turned on your last girlfriend; it might have been the guacamole.

Microwave bacon until crisp, using paper towels to absorb grease.

Cut avocado in half with a sharp knife.

Mash avocado in bowl, then stir in lemon juice, salt and pepper.

Spread avocado mixture onto bread slices.

Add bacon slices.

Put sandwiches in a plastic bag.

Cook time **30 seconds** *Prep time* **20 minutes**

♡ One hour before: Microwave bacon in paper towels. Make avocado mixture; refrigerate in covered glass bowl. Pack picnic basket with crackers, napkins, glasses, plates and serving and eating utensils.

♡ Just before picnic: Mix fruit. Make sandwiches and put cheese and drinks in basket.

SHOPPING LIST

Gourmet Cheese Section
cheddar cheese
camembert
crackers that are sturdy

CHEESE AND CRACKERS

Select an assortment of cheeses from the deli section, possibly a simple Farmer cheese and a soft Camembert. The gourmet cheese section of the grocery store has lots of choices and better crackers that are also sturdy. If you have a small cutting board, take it along. It can be used for cutting and serving. If not, take a small plate. A sharp knife is needed.

Produce
2 fresh peaches
1 cup fresh blueberries

SLICED PEACHES AND BLUEBERRIES

Wash and slice peaches.

Wash blueberries.

Mix together.

Take a bowl for serving or use a plastic container as a serving dish.

*Prep time **5 minutes***

Produce
1/4 watermelon or container of
watermelon pieces
1 cup fresh blueberries

WATERMELON AND BLUEBERRIES

Combine watermelon pieces with blueberries.

Put fruit in a plastic bag or container.

Take a bowl for serving or use plastic container as a serving dish.

*Prep time **5 minutes***

bottled water
iced tea
pinot noir for drinking

BEVERAGES

Sam wants to surprise Barb with a picnic in the woods. He hides the picnic basket before their bike ride. Unfortunately, Sam has trouble finding the hidden basket and they look for the basket for what seems like hours. While this adds lots of laughs, especially to those hearing the story later, you might want to leave a breadcrumb or pine cone trail to the hidden basket.

Autumn Biking Picnic

Pear and Cheese Pockets, Dried Fruit and Nut Mix, Tomatoes, Basil and Mozzarella, Oatmeal Cookies and Hot Apple Cider with Cinnamon Schnapps or English Port or Sauterne

SHOPPING LIST

Produce
1 ripe pear, sliced

Grocery
¹/₄ cup chopped walnuts

Dairy
1 ounce Stilton or blue cheese, crumbled

Bakery
2 pita breads

SHOPPING LIST

Produce
1 large ripe tomato, sliced
¹/₄ cup fresh basil leaves, chopped

Grocery
¹/₄ teaspoon salt
dash of freshly ground black pepper
2 tablespoons olive oil

Dairy
4 ounces mozzarella cheese

Bakery
¹/₄ loaf crusty Italian bread, have the bakery slice it for you

PEAR AND CHEESE POCKETS

Cut pita bread in half through the center.

Open each half to make a pocket.

Combine pear slices in a bowl with Stilton or blue cheese, and chopped walnuts.

Mix together.

Spoon pear mixture into pita pockets.

Put pockets in a plastic bag.

*Prep time **15 minutes***

♡ One hour before: Combine tomatoes, cheese and basil. Refrigerate in glass or plastic covered container. Pack picnic basket with wine, wine opener, bread, fruit and nut mix, napkins, glasses, plates and utensils.

♡ Just before picnic: Make sandwiches.

TOMATOES, BASIL AND CHEESE

In the book *Secrets of Venus*, Vera Lee writes that wives with straying husbands were told to powder their breasts with pulverised basil. If you want your prospective lover to only have eyes for you, first try sprinkling basil on the tomatoes. The aromatic fragrance of the basil is enchanting.

Combine tomatoes, cheese, basil, salt and pepper in a plastic container.

Drizzle olive oil over tomatoes.

Spoon tomato mixture onto a slice of bread just before eating.

*Prep time **10 minutes***

DRIED FRUIT AND NUT MIX

This is especially good for a fall bike ride. Many stores have dried fruits and nuts in bulk. There you can also find dried pineapple, figs, bananas, apples and many varieties of nuts. You can also buy pre-mixed trail mix.

Grocery
¹/₂ cup dried apricots
¹/₄ cup dried cherries
¹/₂ cup whole unblanched almonds
¹/₂ cup cashews

Mix nuts and fruits in a bowl.

Put mixture in a plastic bag or brown paper bag.

Either bag can be used as a serving container; just **roll** down the sides of the bag.

Prep time **5 minutes**

> *"You have to eat oatmeal or you dry up. Anybody knows that."*
>
> Kay Thompson

SHOPPING LIST

Grocery
1/2 cup granulated sugar (white)
3/4 cup packed brown sugar
1 teaspoon vanilla
1 1/2 cups white flour
1 teaspoon baking soda
1 teaspoon cinnamon
1 teaspoon salt
3 cups quick-cooking oats
1 cup raisins

Dairy
1 1/4 cups butter or margarine
1 egg

Liquor
hot apple cider, cinnamon schnapps, port wine, or Sauternes, all for drinking

OATMEAL RAISIN COOKIES

Baking cookies together at your place after the bike ride might be a way to have more fun. You can bake cookies from scratch using the following recipe or you can buy refrigerated cookie dough at the grocery store. While baking cookies, drink hot apple cider with cinnamon schnapps. This cookie baking activity will extend a wonderful afternoon into evening so you can continue intermingling promiscuously on a blanket in front of your fireplace.

Heat oven to 375°F.

Beat butter and sugars until fluffy.

Beat in egg and vanilla.

Add flour, cinnamon, salt and baking soda.

Add oats and raisins; mix.

Drop rounded tablespoons on ungreased baking paper.

Bake 8–9 minutes, until edges are done but centers are soft.

Cool 1 minute on cookie sheet.

Remove to wire rack.

Makes 48. Store in covered container.

Prep time **15 minutes**   *Baking time* **8–9 minutes**

Cook oatmeal for breakfast the next morning. Top with fresh strawberries or bananas, and skim milk.

Picnic Under The Stars In December

FRIED OR BAKED CHICKEN, COLESLAW, POTATO SALAD, LONG ISLAND ICED TEA OR LEMONADE WITH VODKA, PLASTIC ANTS, STARS ON THE CEILING, OCEAN SOUNDS

Buy chicken and salads at the deli section of your grocery store or at Kentucky Fried Chicken.

Setting the Scene: Put a tablecloth or blanket on your bed; use plastic picnic ware; get plastic ants from Michael's and stars from Spencer's that will stick to the ceiling. Serve food in large seashells or children's plastic buckets with toy shovels as serving spoons. Play a CD of ocean sounds while eating your picnic. When you turn off the bedroom lights to watch a movie or listen to 'Moonlight Sonata', she will see the glow-in-the-dark stars on the ceiling and be fascinated. The stars could spell out a message, like "Be Mine". You can put a message in a bottle in the guest bathroom.

Become *one lucky son of the sea*.

♡ One day before: Buy utensils, stars and ants. Put stars on the ceiling.

♡ Just before picnic: Put ants on bed. Pick up food. Refrigerate salads until ready to serve. Keep chicken warm if served right away. If not, refrigerate and re-heat. Make drinks just before she arrives.

Eric has met the perfect woman; Susie has a wonderful sense of humor and is lots of fun. She even wants the kind of relationship that most men want: while apart, each can do whatever they want with no questions asked. To Eric, this is perfect. After six months, Eric wants more of a commitment and plans a picnic in his bedroom in December. With stars on the ceiling and a message in the bottle, Eric seals the deal on a long-term committed relationship with Susie.

After Cross-country Skiing

If this is your first time cross-country skiing, start with a small country.

BLACK BEANS AND RICE, FRESH-BAKED FRENCH BREAD, BREAD PUDDING, AND IRISH COFFEE OR HOT COCOA WITH COFFEE LIQUEUR

After a morning of skiing, head to your home or cabin for hearty food and great times.

SHOPPING LIST

Produce
1 ripe tomato, chopped (optional)
1/2 red onion, chopped (optional)
1 avocado, sliced

Grocery
7 ounce package of black beans and rice
tortilla chips, preferably blue (crumble chips to bite-size)

Meat
1/2 pound sausage (pork or turkey), ground, or sweet Italian sausage (optional)

Miscellaneous
2 thermoses
paper towels

BLACK BEANS AND RICE

Beans are among the oldest foods knows to humanity, dating back at least four thousand years. Famed trumpeter Louis Armstrong loved beans so much that he signed his letters with their praise:

> *Red beans and ricely yours.*
>
> Louis Armstrong (his sign-off on personal letters)

Cook beans and rice according to package directions.

If adding Italian sausage, **slice** into 2–4 inch pieces and **cook** in a small skillet.

If adding ground sausage, **crumble** it into a frying-pan and cook.

Absorb grease on paper towels.

Add sausage to black beans and rice.

Pour beans and rice into a thermos if picnic will be on the slopes.

Prep time **10 minutes**   *Cook time* **15 minutes**

♡ One day before: Put bread in picnic basket along with napkins, utensils, plates and glasses. Make the bread pudding and whiskey sauce. Fry sausage.

♡ One hour before: Make black beans and rice.

♡ 30 minutes before: Make Irish coffee or hot cocoa and put it in thermos.

Take cups and spoons. Garnishes are optional but do add flavor and interest. If taking sliced tomato, chopped onion, avocados and tortilla chips, put them in separate plastic bags or plastic containers.

FRESH-BAKED FRENCH BREAD

Serve in the rolled down bag that the bread comes in.

Take butter and knife

BREAD PUDDING

Bread pudding can be made ahead and re-heated after you return from skiing. You and your skiing partner can make the pudding and whiskey sauce together as an after skiing activity. Drink Irish coffee while cooking. It will quickly warm you up after skiing. Buy Irish whiskey and Irish Cream if you don't know which your date prefers. Don't forget the whipped cream.

Preheat oven to 350°F. **Put** bread slices in rectangular baking pan.

Mix together milk, whole eggs, egg yolks, sugar and vanilla.

Melt butter and **pour** over bread. **Pour** milk mixture over bread, letting bread absorb the liquid.

In larger baking pan or dish, **fill** half way with water. **Set** smaller baking dish that has pudding mixture into the dish with water.

Place pans in oven and bake for 45 minutes.

Serve warm and top with whiskey sauce.

*Prep time **10 minutes** Cook time **45 minutes***

Grocery
$^{1}/_{2}$ cup sugar

Dairy
5 large egg yolks

Liquor
$^{1}/_{4}$ cup Irish Whiskey or bourbon

Miscellaneous
double boiler or two saucepans
(one large and one small)

WHISKEY SAUCE

Beat egg yolks and sugar in a bowl using an electric mixer.

Add whiskey and beat until well mixed.

Transfer mixture to top of a double boiler, with cold water in the bottom. Mixture can be in a smaller saucepan and set in a larger pan that has cold water in it.

Cook, stirring constantly, over medium-high heat until water in the bottom pot starts to boil and mixture is thick and creamy.

Serve hot or cold. **Whisk** before serving.

*Prep time **5 minutes** Cook time **5–10 minutes***

Brad meets Janel when flying to Colorado for a skiing vacation. She is everything Brad likes in a woman – intelligent, petite, pretty, witty and a skier. They talk, laugh, watch a movie and fall in love at 30,000 feet. As they get off the plane, Janel says "see you at the baggage carousel." Brad chokes while getting his luggage and doesn't find out where she is staying.
As he drives away in his rental car, he initially rationalizes that it is geography; he lives in Chicago and she lives in New Jersey. But the real reason is fear of rejection.

He knows that most invitations and overtures of love flatter women, but Brad again forgets this at a critical opportunity. He also knows that unlike streetcars, another Janel will not come along in 20 minutes.

Brad runs into Janel on the ski slopes and skis with her for the rest of the day. He invites her to go dancing after skiing. The next day they cross-country ski and have this picnic where they fall in love at 5,000 feet.

"Only Irish coffee provides in a single glass all four essential food groups:
alcohol, caffeine, sugar, and fat."

Alex Levine

SHOPPING LIST

Grocery
dark roast coffee beans, ground

Liquor
Irish cream

Miscellaneous
thermos

COFFEE WITH IRISH CREAM

Coffee with Irish Cream is also a great after-skiing drink. You can drink it while making the bread pudding and whiskey sauce.

Make coffee.

Put 4 cups of coffee in a thermos, if you take it skiing.

Add 8 shots of Irish cream.

Prep time **5–10 minutes**

SHOPPING LIST

Grocery
dark roast coffee beans, ground
4 teaspoons of sugar

Dairy
whipped cream

Liquor
4 shots Irish whiskey

Miscellaneous
thermos

IRISH COFFEE WITH IRISH WHISKEY

Make coffee.

Put 4 cups in thermos. **Mix** sugar and whiskey, thoroughly dissolving the sugar.

Add whiskey and sugar to coffee.

Top with whipped cream just before serving.

Prep time **5–10 minutes**

5.2 Before Theatre Appetizers

"An interesting appetizer and bottle of wine,
the second and third best things in life."

adapted from *Paint Your Wagon*

Astound your date with one of these inviting appetizers before any special event such as the theatre, a concert, a basketball game, etc. Whichever one you choose, it will transform your evening from ordinary to exceptional. Select a wine that complements the appetizer. Remember the scene in *Paint Your Wagon* where Ben (Lee Marvin) exposes the church-going family's son to his first sex, whiskey and cigar. At dinner that night, Horton tells his parents, "if you haven't had whiskey and a good cigar, you are missing the second and third best things in life." The right appetizer and wine can turn an evening into a night to remember.

SHOPPING LIST

Dairy
1 small round or wedge of Brie

Bakery
1 baguette (have bakery slice)

Liquor
chardonnay, riesling, or
gwertztramener

Grocery
strawberry jam

SHOPPING LIST

Produce
jalapeño, chopped

Grocery
¹/₂ cup peach jam
triscuits

Dairy
goat cheese
montrachet
1 tablespoon butter

TO BRIE OR NOT TO BRIE
BAGUETTES AND WINE

Take Brie out of refrigerator about two hours before serving as it is best at room temperature. Using a knife, poke holes in the brie, fill with strawberry jam. Heat a few minutes in microwave.

Surround Brie with baguettes.

A small knife is needed to **cut** the Brie.

*Prep time **2 hours***

MONTRACHET TOPPED WITH PEACH PEPPER JAM

Place cheese on serving plate.

Sauté jalapeño in butter. Add to peach jam, pour over cheese.

Microwave for 30 seconds, until warmed through.

Surround cheese with crackers and serve.

(recipe on page 157)

SHOPPING LIST

Deli
¹/₂ quart chicken salad

Produce
1 tablespoon cilantro

Bakery
crusty wholewheat bread

Liquor
sauvignon blanc, chardonnay to drink

Grocery
sesame oil

SESAME CHICKEN SALAD, BREAD AND WINE (above)

Pour a glass of wine.

Mix sesame oil and cilantro with chicken salad.

Serve with bread or crackers.

*Prep time **15 minutes, refrigerate overnight***

♡ One day before: Mix chicken salad, cilantro and sesame oil. Taste; add more sesame oil if you want a stronger flavor. Refrigerate in glass or plastic container.

♡ 30 minutes before: Take chicken out of refrigerator. Slice bread if serving bread.

SHOPPING LIST

Produce
3 ripe medium avocados
1¹/₂ tablespoons lemon juice

Grocery
blue tortilla chips
caviar for garnish (optional)

Dairy
1¹/₂ ounces Roquefort or blue cheese, crumbled
2 tablespoons heavy cream

Liquor
chardonnay or semillon–chardonnay blend to drink

AVOCADO MOUSSE AND TORTILLA CHIPS WITH WINE

Pour a glass of wine.

Halve avocados; **remove** and **discard** seeds.

Scoop flesh from skins using a spoon.

Mash avocados with a fork.

Crumble Roquefort and stir in, along with lemon juice and cream.

Stir until mixture is thoroughly blended.

Refrigerate, **covered**, for at least an hour or overnight.

Fifteen minutes before serving, **remove** from refrigerator and stir.

Serve in a bowl with caviar on top. **Set** bowl in the middle of a plate and **put** tortilla chips around the edge.

Prep time **15 minutes**

♡ One day before: Make mousse and refrigerate in a covered glass or plastic container.

♡ 15 minutes before: Remove from refrigerator and stir. Top with caviar. Surround with tortilla chips.

SHOPPING LIST

Grocery
7 ounces sun-dried tomatoes in oil, undrained
1 box crackers

Dairy
8 ounces cream cheese, softened
¹/₂ cup Parmesan cheese

Liquor
chardonnay or pinot noir to drink

SUN-DRIED TOMATO SPREAD AND WINE

Drain oil from sun-dried tomatoes.

Blend tomatoes, cream cheese and Parmesan.

Pour into a serving bowl. Serve with crackers.

Prep time **10 minutes**

♡ One day before: Make sun-dried tomato spread. Refrigerate overnight in covered container.

♡ 30 minutes before: Take out of refrigerator and put in serving bowl.

SHOPPING LIST

Produce
8 ounces fresh mushrooms
$^1/_2$ onion, chopped
1–2 teaspoons minced garlic

Grocery
2 tablespoons olive oil
$^1/_2$ cup walnuts

Dairy
4 ounces Farmer cheese

Bakery
1 baguette

Liquor
$^1/_4$ cup pinot noir for recipe,
rest for drinking

MUSHROOM PÂTÉ WITH WINE (above)

Pour a glass of wine.

Sauté mushrooms and chopped onion in olive oil.

Add garlic, $^1/_4$ cup of wine and cheese.

Cover saucepan with lid and turn off heat so cheese will soften.

Blend in blender or food processor.

Refrigerate.

Just before serving, **add** walnuts and blend quickly so walnuts will be coarsely ground.

Serve in a bowl with baguettes.

Prep time **15 minutes**   *Cook time* **10 minutes**

♡ One day before: Make pâté, combining all ingredients except walnuts. Leave in blender.

♡ One hour before: Take pâté from refrigerator and add walnuts. Scrape pâté into serving bowl. Surround pâté with baguettes.

> *"The brief emergence (of morels) coincides with the season of rebirth and beauty, when Nature springs awake with a sweeping mandate for all her subjects to breed. Seeking morels during this time puts lead in your pencil."*
>
> John Ratzloff

SHOPPING LIST

Produce
1 tablespoon chives, chopped

Dairy
6 ounces cream cheese, softened
2 tablespoons milk or sour cream

1/2 teaspoon horseradish (optional)

Seafood
1/2 cup smoked salmon, flaked

Grocery
crackers

Liquor
chardonnay or champagne to drink
2 tablespoons champagne

SALMON SPREAD AND CRACKERS WITH WINE

Most delis have delicious smoked salmon spreads in regular and Cajun style.

Pour a glass of champagne.

Mix cream cheese, milk or sour cream, chives, salmon, champagne and horseradish thoroughly.

Spoon into a bowl.

Refrigerate overnight.

Serve with crackers.

Prep time **10 minutes**

♡ One day before: Make salmon spread. Refrigerate in a glass or plastic container, covered.

♡ One hour before: Take salmon spread out of the refrigerator and put it into a serving bowl or plate. Surround with crackers.

Phil had dated several women who live by the rules and are always on a low-fat sugar-free diet. Not only was it difficult to schedule a date, but serving food that meets their dietary needs of the moment was as difficult as finding a flea on an elephant's ass. Being questioned over every entrée ingredient and method of preparation totally takes away the joy of eating. Then Phil sees his dream girl eating alone in his favorite cafe. Kim orders a BLT without asking the cholesterol content of the mayonnaise or the number of grains in the bread. Phil introduces himself to Kim, asks if she would like to go to the theatre on Saturday night, and come to his place first for an appetizer and a glass of wine. They exchange business cards, home and cell telephone numbers and addresses. This is the beginning of a great summer relationship where they share their passion for passion.

5.3 AFTER DINNER CHERRY-POPPING DESSERTS

These desserts are deliciously decadent and are from the pre-calorie-counting era. Invite her to your place for dessert and coffee. Show her your art collection and without a word, tell her she is art.

Men are like desserts: something most women could live very well without and still have a very full life. Many of the women you date have been on a diet since they were 10; lifetime members of Undereaters Anonymous. Your date will fall off the wagon for the right decadent dessert.

The recipes in this chapter are simple and won't keep you in the kitchen puffing pastries while your date is sitting patiently in the living room. A simpler option, select several desserts from the gourmet dessert section of the grocery store.

CHOCOLATE BREAD PUDDING (recipe on page 162)

SHOPPING LIST

Grocery

1 tablespoon vanilla

6 ounces dark chocolate chips

2 tablespoons sugar

Dairy

2 cups milk

1/2 cup sour cream

4 egg yolks

Bakery

1/2 loaf sliced white bread with crusts removed

CHOCOLATE BREAD PUDDING (photograph on page 161)

After eating this dessert, your date will whisper that she loves you more than chocolate: the ultimate compliment.

Heat oven to 300°F.

Place milk and vanilla in medium saucepan; **whisk** together until smooth.

Gently **heat** until nearly boiling.

Add chocolate and **whisk** until smooth.

Combine egg yolks and sugar in a large bowl and whisk.

Pour chocolate mixture very slowly into egg-yolk mixture, whisking constantly until fully combined.

Line baking dish with bread slices so they are two deep.

Slowly **pour** chocolate custard over bread, making sure all bread is soaked. Wait 30 minutes before baking.

Place baking dish in a larger pan; **fill** outer pan with hot water halfway up the sides of the dish.

Bake until set (about 30 minutes). **Cool** for 15 minutes. This bread pudding can be baked ahead and re-heated when ready to serve.

Serve bread pudding warm topped with sour cream.

Prep time **45 minutes**   *Cook time* **30 minutes**

♡ One day before: Make bread pudding.

♡ 15 minutes before: Re-heat pudding. Make lattes.

SHOPPING LIST

Grocery
3/4 cup pecans or walnuts
1/2 cup chocolate sauce
(a quality ice cream topping)

Frozen Desserts
1 pint coffee ice cream

CHOCOLATE-COFFEE SUNDAES

Heat chocolate in the microwave for 10 seconds.

Scoop coffee ice cream into bowls.

Top with chocolate sauce and nuts. Serve.

If you want to make a good chocolate sauce, use the recipe below.

Prep time **5 minutes**

♡ One day before: If making sauce, make it then.

♡ 10 minutes before: Take ice cream out of freezer. Heat chocolate sauce. Make sundaes.

SHOPPING LIST

Grocery
3 ounces semi-sweet chocolate

Dairy
1/4 cup thickened cream

CHOCOLATE SAUCE

Bring cream to boil over medium heat in a heavy saucepan.

Remove from heat and **add** chocolate.

Stir until smooth. **Cover** to keep warm.

Prep time **5 minutes**   *Cook time* **5 minutes**

SHOPPING LIST

1 package raspberry mousse mix
fresh raspberries

RASPBERRY MOUSSE

Make mousse according to package directions.

Refrigerate in covered plastic or glass bowl.

Wash raspberries and drain in colander.

Pour mousse into small bowls and top with fresh raspberries.

Grocery
4 tablespoons brown sugar
¹/₂ cup pecans

Frozen Desserts
1 frozen apple pie
1 pint vanilla ice cream

Dairy
4 ounces butter

HOW DO YOU LIKE THEM APPLES PIE?

When you taste this pie, you will know that you have hit culinary gold. Buying a frozen apple pie and baking it according to directions with or without the caramel topping, is also delightful. Just don't forget the vanilla ice cream.

Take frozen pie out of baking tin.

Pour butter, brown sugar and pecans into the baking tin.

Put frozen pie back in baking tin.

Bake according to directions.

When baked, **put** a dinner plate on top of pie and hold tight.

Turn it over and pie will drop onto the plate.

Scrape the caramel sauce onto the pie.

This pie can be **baked** ahead and **re-heated** just before serving.

Serve with vanilla ice cream.

Prep time **10 minutes**   *Cook time* **According to package**

Produce
2 bananas

Grocery
2 tablespoons brown sugar
¹/₈ teaspoon cinnamon

Dairy
2 tablespoons butter

Frozen Desserts
1 pint vanilla ice cream

Liquor
¹/₄ cup dark rum for recipe

Miscellaneous
long matches

YES, I HAVE GREAT BANANAS FOSTER

This dessert would be a great afternoon delight.

Peel bananas.

Cut bananas in half, lengthwise.

Melt butter in small frying-pan over medium heat.

Add brown sugar and cinnamon and stir well.

Add bananas and sauté until bananas are slightly soft (about 1–2 minutes per side).

Pour rum into the pan, heat for 1 minute and then ignite using a long match.

When flames burn out, **place** bananas in two serving dishes. **Top** with ice cream and sauce from the bottom of the pan.

Prep time **5 minutes**   *Cook time* **5–6 minutes**

SHOPPING LIST

Produce
1 fresh pear, apple and peach
6 fresh apricots

Grocery
¹/₂ cup whole pecans

Deli
1 wedge or small round of Brie

Liquor
1 bottle of chardonnay to drink

SHOPPING LIST

Grocery
espresso coffee beans (decaf.)

Dairy
skim milk

Special Equipment
espresso machine
coffee grinder

BRIE, NUTS, FRUIT AND CHARDONNAY

Before going out for the evening, **take** Brie out of the refrigerator.

Wash fruit, core and slice fruit just before serving.

Surround Brie with fruits and nuts.

Prep time **10 minutes**

SKINNY LATTES

Grind coffee beans.

Make coffee.

Steam milk.

Prep time **5 minutes**

Henry meets Maureen at a gallery opening in Seattle. Henry is an investment banker and Maureen is an editor. Maureen has just extricated herself from Infidelity Man with no intention of getting involved with any more men. Falling in love has a short shelf life and for Maureen the end is excruciating. She is especially reluctant to get involved with Henry, who seems to be the ultimate guy. She needs a regular guy. Since both are supporters of the arts, they run into each other at several functions. Henry finally convinces Maureen to go with him to the theatre. Afterwards he invites her to dessert at his place. After two helpings of chocolate bread pudding and a grande latte, she realizes that whether it lasts a moment, an hour, an afternoon, a year or a lifetime, relationships are still great. Henry and Maureen just celebrated their six-month anniversary.

CHICKEN AND RICE SALAD
(recipe on page 167)

5.4 AFTER WORKING OUT (AN EXERCISE IN GOOD TASTE)

After working out together, at home or gym, invite her for dinner and prepare one of these healthy salads. Your grocery store may have a deli with intriguing salads. Select a couple of the healthier, yet interesting choices. Serve salad with crusty whole grain bread and olive oil, unless otherwise specified. After a hot shower and this meal, the heavy breathing you heard earlier at the gym may again be heard in your bedroom. The human body has over 45 miles of nerves. Enjoy the ride.

All of the salads include low-fat proteins, essential for a healthier, happier, longer sex life. A low protein diet inhibits sexuality.

CHICKEN AND RICE SALAD (opposite)

Cook rice according to package directions; substitute chicken broth for water. **Drain**.

Transfer drained rice to a bowl and squeeze half a lemon over rice. **Stir** rice. **Cool**.

Add chicken, onions, red pepper and sugar snap peas to rice.

Toss with dressing (see below); cover and refrigerate for at least 2 hours. This can be made the day before. Just before serving, **add** avocado and pecans. **Toss** to blend.

Serve in serving bowl.

Prep time **15 minutes**   *Cook time* **45 minutes**

♡ Day before: Make salad.

♡ 30 minutes before serving: Add avocado and pecans.

♡ 5 minutes before serving: Heat bread and grind pepper over olive oil.

DRESSING

Blend ingredients for dressing in blender or **mix** thoroughly in a mixing bowl. **Pour** over salad and mix well.

Serve salad with crusty bread and olive oil (recipe on page 169).

Prep time **5 minutes**

*"A diet that consists predominantly of rice
leads to the use of opium."*

Friedrich Nietzsche

Produce

1 tablespoon lime juice, from fresh lime

3 tablespoons cilantro leaves, minced

1 jalapeño pepper, cored and seeded

1 teaspoon minced garlic

1/4 cup cucumber, chopped

1/4 red onion, sliced

1 avocado, pitted, peeled and diced

Grocery

1 tablespoon olive oil

1/4 teaspoon salt

1/8 teaspoon sugar

3 tablespoons balsamic vinegar

15 ounce can black beans, drained

SHOPPING LIST

Produce
1 lime

Beverages
club soda

Miscellaneous
ice

SHOPPING LIST

Refrigerated Section
1 tube cornbread sticks

BLACK BEAN AND AVOCADO SALAD

St. Jerome divided his beans among the hungry, but gave none to his nuns as beans excite genital titillation.

Pour lime juice into blender or mixing bowl.

Add oil, 2 tablespoons cilantro, jalapeño pepper, garlic, salt, sugar and balsamic vineger.

Blend or stir until smooth.

Mix beans, cucumber, onion and 1 tablespoon cilantro.

Just before serving, **pour** dressing over bean mixture and **add** avocado.

Prep time **15 minutes**

♡ Day before: Make dressing. Store dressing in refrigerator.

♡ 1 hour before: Mix beans, cucumber, onion and cilantro. Make cornbread.

♡ 15 minutes before: Pour dressing over beans.

CLUB SODA WITH SLICES OF LIME

Slice limes and put on the glass.

Add ice.

Pour club soda over ice.

Serve.

CORNBREAD STICKS

They are good at room temperature, so can be made day before and stored in airtight container. If you cannot find cornbread sticks, substitute package of cornbread or frozen cornbread.

Bake according to directions.

Bake the day before and store in airtight container.

> *"I say it's spinach, and I say the hell with it."*
>
> E. B. White

Spinach and Grilled Chicken (photograph on page 170)

Spinach is one of the healthiest greens you can eat. It is known to be a preventive for everything from cancer to cataracts. Just don't count on it building "muscles" as it did for Popeye when defending Olive Oil's honor against Bluto.

Mix spinach, mushrooms, red pepper, tomatoes and chicken strips in a large bowl.

Slice red onion and separate into rings.

Pour spinach into a serving bowl and top with onion rings.

Heat spinach salad dressing in microwave

Drizzle dressing over salad.

Serve salad with tongs.

*Prep time **10 minutes**   Cook time **10 minutes***

♡ One hour before: Combine spinach, onion, mushrooms, tomatoes and chicken strips. Cover bowl and refrigerate.

♡ 15 minutes before: Top with croutons and drizzle dressing over salad. Heat bread and grind pepper over olive oil.

Crusty Bread and Olive Oil Topped with Black Pepper

Pepper was once so rare and considered so valuable that it was used as currency. The rich kept large quantities of pepper in their houses. A poor person was said to lack pepper. It is now inexpensive, plentiful and no longer a measure of one's wealth.

Preheat oven to 300°F.

Warm bread for 10 minutes.

Cut into $^1/_2$ inch thick slices.

Serve oil in small, shallow bowl. **Grind** pepper over the oil. You will need two bread plates.

TAE-BO OR NOT TAE-BO??

James and Meredith meet at a fitness center. While jogging on treadmills, they talk about their similar passions – biking, roller-blading, rock climbing, running, swimming, golf and beach volleyball. After working out, James invites Meredith to his place for salad and crusty bread. Later that evening, James puts on a full court press and lights up her loafers. They discover their mutual interest in indoor sports and multiple yogasms.

5.5 ROMANCING THE SOUP

Spend a Sunday afternoon by visiting real estate open houses, especially expensive new "dream homes". This is a good way to find out your date's tastes and lifestyle expectations. Afterwards, go to your place for a Sunday soup supper and watch television. Soup is the ultimate comfort food. A bowl of hot, hearty soup is a great wintertime meal. Just add a hunk of bread and possibly a salad. No alcohol as Monday is a work day.

Take your bowls of soup to bed and assuming you have a television in your bedroom, watch a show, then watch another show while having a second bowl of soup. Bread is preferable to crackers, but don't kick her out of bed if she insists on crackers with her soup. Put bread, butter and a knife in a basket. Place the basket in the bed in between the two of you for "bread in the middle".

While soup making has been elevated to the level of haute cuisine, you can purchase containers of soup from your favorite supermarket or restaurant that has take-out. Make the soup ahead of time and warm the soup in a saucepan after she arrives.

SHOPPING LIST

Produce
2 medium yellow onions, thinly sliced

Grocery
1¹/2 teaspoons oil
1 teaspoon brown sugar
2 cups boiling beef broth
salt and pepper

Dairy
1¹/2 tablespoons butter
grated Gruyère or Parmesan cheese

Liquor
3 tablespoons dry white wine
1 tablespoon brandy (optional), for recipe

Bakery
2 slices French bread

FRENCH ONION SOUP

You could rent a movie and settle down in front of the TV for a warm and intimate evening.

"If your wife is old and

your member is exhausted, eat onions aplenty."

Marital

Heat butter and oil in a heavy based saucepan; add onions and stir.

Cover and cook over low heat until soft (10–12 minutes).

Stir in sugar, cover and continue cooking over moderate heat until onions are a deep golden brown.

Add the broth, wine and seasonings to taste.

Cover and simmer gently for 30 minutes.

Toast the bread slowly in the oven.

Note: Can be made the day before and re-heated. Toast the bread and add the brandy just before serving. Top with cheese.

Serve with slices of French bread and butter.

*Prep time **10 minutes**   Cooking time **45 minutes***

Elizabeth has oral surgery. She is miserable and can only eat liquids and soft foods. Tom insists on coming over and fixing dinner for her. He will bring everything. Tom brings five cans of soup and three boxes of Jell-O. Elizabeth selects tomato soup and orange Jell-O. Tom prepares both and serves them to her. There is nothing like soup to make you feel warm and secure and to recall the love and care felt as a child when your mother and grandmother

> *"If the soup had been as warm as the wine; if the wine had been as cold as the turkey; and if the turkey had had a breast like the maid, it would have been a swell dinner."*
>
> Duncan Hines

made pots of soup. What Tom did wasn't really anything, but Elizabeth was totally impressed that he did it all. Elizabeth will long remember the warmth of the soup along with Tom's thoughtful planning of this evening.

SHOPPING LIST

Produce
1 leek
1 teaspoon minced garlic
2 medium baking potatoes
1 tablespoon fresh parsley, chopped

Grocery
2 teaspoons olive oil
$1/2$ teaspoon salt and pepper
20 ounces chicken broth

Dairy
2 teaspoons butter
$1/2$ cup whipping cream
$1/4$ cup Parmesan cheese

CREAMY POTATO AND LEEK SOUP

Cut off the dark-green part of the leeks as well as the roots.

Rinse leek very well as some are sandy.

Cut leeks into 2 inch slices.

Heat oil and butter in a large pot over medium heat.

Add leeks and garlic; **cook**, **covered**, for about 5–7 minutes or until leeks are tender and translucent.

Peel potatoes and cut into $1/2$ inch pieces.

Add broth, potatoes, salt and pepper to the pot with leeks.

Bring to boil, **reduce** heat to simmer, and **cook** uncovered for 25 minutes or until potatoes are tender.

Remove from heat and mash some of the potatoes to thicken the soup.

Add milk, Parmesan and parsley.

Reheat on medium-low heat.

Ladle into soup bowls.

Prep time **10 minutes**   *Cook time* **30 minutes**

Serve with slices of French bread and butter.

SHOPPING LIST

Produce
1 red pepper
6 green onions, chopped
$^1/_2$ cup celery, chopped
1 teaspoons garlic, minced

Grocery
4 tablespoons oil
4 cups chicken broth
$^1/_8$ teaspoon cayenne pepper
$^1/_2$ cup long grain rice

Dairy
4 tablespoons butter

Meat/Seafood
1 cup chicken breast, cut in chunks
$^1/_2$ cup andouille sausages
$^1/_2$ cup peeled and deveined shrimp

SHOPPING LIST

Grocery
honey

Dairy
butter

Frozen Foods
cornbread

JAMBALAYA SOUP

In a heavy pan, **melt** butter and oil over low heat.

Brown the onions, then **add** celery, red pepper and garlic. **Cook** for 5 minutes, stirring constantly.

Add the chicken and sausage, continue to cook over low heat, stirring constantly for about 15 minutes.

Add shrimp and cayenne pepper, stirring constantly for 5 minutes more.

Add rice and chicken broth, cook over low heat for 45 minutes covered, uncovering from time to time to stir.

Prep time **15 minutes** *Cook time* **1$^1/_2$ hours**

Make the day before and reheat before serving.

CORNBREAD, BUTTER AND HONEY

Serve cornbread on a plate and **arrange** small pots of honey and butter on the side.

Hippocrates prescribed honey to anxiety-ridden grooms-to-be in the fifth century BC (hence the origin of the word "honeymoon"). According to legend, Attila the Hun slurped so much honey wine on his wedding night that he OD'd. The Egyptians offered honey to the god of fertility, Min. If the pictures of his erection are accurate, give honey a try. Your honey will be grateful if it works.

> *"If envious age relax the nuptial knot,*
> *Thy food be mushrooms, And thy feast be shallot."*
>
> Marital

SHOPPING LIST

Produce
3 tablespoons minced onion
bunch of parsley
1 pound sliced mushrooms
$1/3$ teaspoon lemon juice

Grocery
2 tablespoons flour
4 cups chicken broth
dash of salt

Dairy
3 tablespoons butter
$1/3$ cup thickened cream

MUSHROOM SOUP

> *"Mushrooms are like men –*
> *the bad most closely counterfeit the good."*
>
> George Ellwanger

Cook onions in $1^1/2$ tablespoons butter until soft.

Stir in flour and cook over low heat for 4 minutes without browning.

Add broth, blending it completely with flour.

Add parsley and simmer for 20 minutes.

Melt remaining butter in large pan.

In a skillet mushrooms in butter with salt and lemon juice and **cook** for 5 minutes. If not to be used immediately, set aside.

Reheat to simmer.

Add cream to soup and heat through.

Taste for seasoning.

Serve immediately garnished with chopped parsley.

Prep time **10 minutes**   *Cook time* **25 minutes**

Blonde and Beautiful 127 met Young Architect in an over-30 chat room and they became virtual friends. After several weeks of daily emails they meet for coffee. Each had given their actual age, gender, height and weight. Randy (Young Architect) considered trimming a few years from his age and several inches from his waist as he anticipated that B & B hadn't filled him in on every last bit of her cellulate. He was more concerned that meeting would turn their great cyberspace relationship to saccharine. Lisa (B&B) was afraid Randy would be totally different from his description. Lisa meets Randy's most important expectation and turn for a man: she shows up. Both look as

they described themselves and Randy gave no indication of mental or criminal tendencies. After three hours of coffee and conversation they decide to see each other again, realizing that on the Internet, you don't hear a human voice or get a hug. Randy invited Lisa to a Sunday afternoon matinee and cybersoup at his place. They watch TV and listen to his romantic CDs. They are now living together.

SHOPPING LIST

Produce
1/2 clove garlic, cut in half

Grocery
salt and freshly ground pepper
3 tablespoons best quality extra-virgin olive oil

Bakery
4 slices country bread

BASIC BRUSCHETTA (above)

Toast or grill bread.

Rub one side of warm bread with garlic clove.

Sprinkle lightly with salt and pepper.

Drizzle with oil.

Serve immediately. Instead of bruschetta, you could also buy sourdough, focaccia or a grainy wholemeal bread.

*Prep time **5 minutes**   Cooking time **2–5 minutes***

Index